THE LAIRD OF DRAMMOCHDYLE

AUP titles of related interest

POPULAR LITERATURE IN VICTORIAN SCOTLAND
Language, fiction and the press
William Donaldson

GRAMPIAN HAIRST
An Anthology of Northeast Prose
Edited by William Donaldson and Douglas Young

DAVID RORIE Poems and Prose
Edited by William Donaldson

TEN MODERN SCOTTISH NOVELS
Isobel Murray and Bob Tait

LITERATURE OF THE NORTH
Edited by David Hewitt and Michael Spiller

THE CLYACK SHEAF
Sketches of Life and Characters in Northeast Scotland
David Toulmin

A BLASPHEMER AND REFORMER
A Study of Lewis Grassic Gibbon
William K. Malcolm

FROM THE CLYDE TO CALIFORNIA
Robert Louis Stevenson
Edited and Introduced by Andrew Noble

THE LUM HAT AND OTHER STORIES
Last tales of Violet Jacob
Edited by Ronald Garden

THE CONCISE SCOTS DICTIONARY
A comprehensive one-volume dictionary of the Scots
Language from the 12th Century to the present day
Editor-in-chief Mairi Robinson

THE LAIRD OF DRAMMOCHDYLE
AND HIS CONTEMPORARIES

or
Random Sketches Done in Outline
with a Burnt Stick

WILLIAM ALEXANDER

with an Introduction by
William Donaldson

ABERDEEN UNIVERSITY PRESS

First published 1986
Aberdeen University Press
A member of the Pergamon Group

© Introduction William Donaldson 1986

The publisher acknowledges subsidy from the Scottish
Arts Council towards the publication of this volume.

British Library Cataloguing in Publication Data

Alexander, William, *1826–1894*
    The Laird of Drammochdyle and his
    contemporaries, or, Random sketches done
    in outline with a burnt stick.
    I. Title
    823'.8[F]   PR4044.A12/
ISBN 0 08 034520 4
ISBN 0 08 034521 2 (Pbk)

Printed in Great Britain
The University Press
Aberdeen

CONTENTS

EDITORIAL PREFACE

I discovered *The Laird of Drammochdyle* lurking in serial form amongst back files of the *Aberdeen Free Press* while working on a general study of Scottish newspapers and popular culture (published by AUP 1986 with the title *Popular Literature in Victorian Scotland*). I knew William Alexander as the author of only one full-length piece of fiction, *Johnny Gibb of Gushetneuk* (Aberdeen 1871) and a handful of short stories which appeared under the title *Life Among my Ain Folk* (Aberdeen 1875). But the newspaper record showed matters in rather a different light. It was clear that he had published a large and varied body of fiction in serial form in the various papers for which he worked from the early 1850s onwards, in what amounted to a long and productive literary career. True he had followed the common Victorian practice of publishing anonymously or under pseudonyms, but it was not difficult to identify his work amongst other fiction appearing in the same source, particularly as the basic clues were provided by the author himself or by sources close to him. For example, what appears to be his last full-length novel, a study of burgh politics in Aberdeen published in the *Weekly Free Press* during 1875 under the title 'My Uncle the Baillie' is actually stated to be 'By the Author of *Johnny Gibb of Gushetneuk*'. His earlier works can be identified either internally or by direct attribution, as in the case of the 40,000 word novella entitled 'The Authentic History of Peter Grundie', a study of urban deprivation and social control which appeared in the *Penny Free Press* in 1855. This is stated to be Alexander's in his obituary in 1894, almost certainly compiled by his brother Henry, then editor of the *Daily Free Press*. His earliest extended work, 'Sketches of Rural Life in Aberdeenshire' appeared serially in the *North of Scotland Gazette* and the *Free Press* in 1852–3 under the pseudonym Rusticus and springs directly from the Mutual Instruction movement in which Alexander was actively involved. It includes a number of anecdotes and character names which crop up again in later works known to be his. Therefore, having a significant body of early and later work, I was able to trace the evolution of his highly distinctive style, and attribute novels of the middle and early mature period like *The Laird of Drammochdyle* and 'Ravenshowe and the Residenters Therein' on internal grounds.

The Laird of Drammochdyle was published serially in the Tuesday edition of the *Free Press* shortly after it started when the paper went bi-weekly in 1865. The original weekly edition continued to come out on Fridays priced at 3*d.* and was intended to have a wide 'regional' readership. The new edition was specifically a city paper, priced at 1*d.* and designed for the rapidly expanding urban upper-working and lower middle classes. Even if there were no other evidence to connect Alexander with the novel, the context alone would strongly suggest his probable authorship. At this period, newspaper fiction was often written by members of staff (i.e. it was not syndicated or 'bought-in') and the editorial team on a paper like the *Free Press* compared with today's standards was tiny, perhaps two or three people at most. The only other person of literary reputation on the staff was William McCombie the editor. He was a widely published political economist and moral philosopher who never once, in the course of a long career, ventured into the field of imaginative literature. The theme of the story concerns the impact of big business and the new capitalist entrepreneurial class upon the values of an older agrarian Scotland. Most of Alexander's writing springs from contemporary social issues, and his radical background gave him, as we shall see, very similar attitudes and beliefs to those we find in the novel. Then there is the suggestive overlap between incidents in the story and events known to have occurred in Alexander's own life. One of the leading characters, Robert Morris, loses a limb in an accident, as Alexander did, and the vivid description of his physical distress, social isolation, and loss of earning power clearly springs from the personal experience of the writer. Morris also rises in life through a rigorous course of self-instruction following the accident, as Alexander did.

Equally convincing, perhaps, is the language, or rather languages, in which the novel is written. The elegant, ironical, slightly mannered English, with its occasional idiosyncracies of word-order and phrase, is palpably Alexander's; while the Scots, although idiomatically less dense than that found in later works, proclaims its author in every line. In *Drammochdyle* there are various elements of Alexander's highly distinctive Scots orthography, as well as at least one unmistakable lexical fingerprint: the word 'starshie' (in Ch. XXXIII), an irregular form of 'stushie/stashie/stishie, a fuss or struggle', which, as the *Scottish National Dictionary* notes, is unique to this writer. The case for attributing the *Laird of Drammochdyle* to William Alexander is overwhelming.

Editorial intervention in the text itself has been kept to a minimum. I have, however, silently corrected obvious spelling and punctuation errors, rectified inconsistencies in chapter numbering, and supplied two chapters (XVI and XXX) with titles absent in the original.

I would like to thank the Leverhulme Trust who financed the research that led to the discovery of this novel, and also the staff of Aberdeen City Library, particularly Miss Helen McKenzie and Mr Andrew Burns of Woodside Library.

INTRODUCTION

The Laird of Drammochdyle and his Contemporaries is a hitherto undiscovered novel by William Alexander, author of *Johnny Gibb of Gushetneuk*, the classic account of nineteenth century North-East rural life, and the acknowledged masterpiece of Victorian Scottish fiction.

Alexander was born in the Garioch, the 'girnal of Aberdeenshire', on 12 June 1826, and was brought up on the farm of Damhead, Pitcaple, within sight of the hill of Bennachie. A serious accident in his early twenties prevented him from further agricultural work, and he went on to earn his living by the pen. Like many other able young men of his generation, he was largely self taught. He found his feet as a writer and public speaker through the Mutual Instruction movement which flourished in the North-East at this time under the direction of the remarkable William McCombie, farmer, philosopher, economist and newspaper editor, who offered Alexander a job in the Autumn of 1852. He eventually succeeded McCombie as editor of the *Aberdeen Free Press*, and went on to become one of the leading professional journalists in Victorian Scotland.

After a lengthy period of stagnation, the Scottish press was entering an era of revolutionary growth. Government restrictions had hitherto ensured that newspapers were expensive and relatively small in circulation. But the repeal of the Stamp Act in 1855 produced a whole new generation of cheap papers operating in a greatly expanded market dominated by upper-working and lower middle-class readers. From being a modest local paper publishing once a week, the *Free Press* rapidly developed into the leading journal in the north of Scotland, appearing daily with a separate weekly edition and an evening paper selling heavily in the city and its immediate surroundings; and this despite formidable competition from the *Aberdeen Journal*, the *People's Journal* and the *Dundee Advertiser*, as well as the new wave of local newspapers like the *Peterhead Sentinel*, the *Buchan Observer*, and the *Huntly Express*, which had come into existence following the repeal of the Stamp. By the end

of the century more than forty different newspapers were being published within the North-East of Scotland alone.

One reason for this was the enormous pool of potential readers in the
region thanks to the high quality of schooling within it. The North-East
was the best educated part of Scotland with the highest comparable
adult literacy rate in Britain. At the same time, when Alexander began
his career, there were relatively few publications for the less well-off,
who tended to rely upon chapbooks—cheap printed collections of tales
and songs, distributed through town and countryside by packmen and
peddlers—for everyday non-devotional reading-matter. The newspaper was the chapbook's successor and, as its readership expanded,
it tended to evolve into a hybrid form mixing news coverage with many
of the functions of a popular literary miscellany.

Library provision was patchy and books were expensive. The novel
in particular was virtually a luxury item which, at a guinea-and-a-half
for a standard first edition, few even of the middle classes could afford
to buy. Most Victorian Scots got their recreational reading from the
popular Scottish press, which published poetry and fiction, biography
and memoirs, history, folklore and popular musicology in enormous
quantities, developing into the major vehicle of the popular culture of
the time.

Scottish papers carried original fiction in serial form throughout the
second half of the nineteenth century and some thousands of Scottish
novels are preserved in this as yet largely unexplored source, among
them the novels of William Alexander, a pioneer of the form and one
of the leading exponents of the new popular fiction.

Like many Scottish writers at this time Alexander consciously
avoided the book as a publication vehicle, and agreed to issue only one
of his novels, *Johnny Gibb*, in cased form, even then reluctantly, at the
insistence of his friends. The British bookmarket was dominated by
London and it was prepared to tolerate vernacular Scots only in a dilute
and standardised form, just as it was prepared to entertain fictional
treatments of Scottish life only in so far as they satisfied English
prejudices and expectations (as we can see in the Kailyard School which
flourished at the end of the century). Alexander, the supreme realist of
nineteenth century Scottish fiction, was determined to represent the
truth about contemporary life as he saw it. The only way he could
manage this, however, was to address himself to a specifically Scottish
audience. And the only way he could reach it was through the columns
of the popular newspaper press, the major medium of written communication still in Scottish hands.

His first extended piece of fiction, 'Sketches of Rural Life in
Aberdeenshire', was based on a series of dialogues in Scots on contemporary social and economic conditions and it ran in the *Free Press* during

the greater part of 1853. Next came 'The Authentic History of Peter Grundie', a study of the plight of the urban poor, which appeared in the columns of the *Penny Free Press* in 1855, and is the earliest novel of substance to be written specifically for publication in a newspaper in Scotland. *The Laird of Drammochdyle* followed in 1865-6, and then in 1867-8, 'Ravenshowe and the Residenters Therein', a study of the pre-capitalist farming community of the Garioch in the opening decades of the nineteenth century. This formed the first stage of Alexander's epic fictional study of the agricultural revolution in Aberdeenshire, spanning almost a hundred years of change, whose central section is formed by *Johnny Gibb of Gushetneuk* (1869-70), and which reaches its conclusion in the later stories of *Life Among my Ain Folk* (first published in the *Free Press* 1872-3). In 'Ravenshowe' the crofters and rural craftsmen enjoy harmonious and uncompetitive relations with one another and with their Scots-speaking laird in a society where everyone knows where they stand, and the distance between social classes is small and clearly defined. *Johnny Gibb* shows the system a generation later with the laird become an absentee and the farmer class split into contending factions, the capitalistic muckle farmers and the smaller tenants of whom Johnny Gibb is the representative and spokesman. The later short stories, 'Mary Malcolmson's Wee Maggie', 'Baubie Huie's Bastard Geet', 'Francie Herregerie's Sharger Laddie' and the brilliant 'Couper Sandy', show the harsh consequences of the new order for the cotters, labourers and smaller tenant farmers. What appears to be Alexander's last full novel, 'My Uncle the Baillie' (1876-7) deals with burgh politics in the city of 'Greyness' (a thinly disguised Aberdeen) and illustrates his continuing interest in urban themes.

William Alexander is a prolific novelist of wide thematic range and considerable variety of style, from austere realism at one end of the scale, to mellow social comedy at the other. Any one of the undiscovered serial novels could have been selected as the first in what is hoped will be an extensive programme of re-publication to mark the centenary of his death in 1994. *The Laird of Drammochdyle* was chosen because it shows the Alexander of the textbooks in an intriguingly unfamiliar light. Here, after all, is not a story about country matters, or religion, or life a generation or so before, but one dealing with major contemporary issues, predominantly urban in its implications, encompassing the whole social range of the community, and possessing, unlike *Johnny Gibb*, a well-defined plot with a powerful denouement.

The Laird of Drammochdyle is a study of power which takes for its theme the destruction of the traditional élite by the rising capitalist bourgeoisie. It is set in the environs of a county town called Strathaven in the North-East of Scotland during the later 1850s, and there are five main characters: firstly Robert Morris, a journeyman carpenter who is disabled at the beginning of the story and eventually rises to modest affluence as partner in a timber-shipping business. He is the main moral focus of the book, intelligent, persevering and unswervingly upright, and it is by his actions that those of the other characters are judged. These include Edward Boyce, the Laird of Drammochdyle, a well-meaning and wealthy young country gentleman, who is systematically debauched by powerful local business interests determined to usurp his position in society, and ends the story impoverished and virtually insane, standing trial for a murder he probably did not commit. Next comes Dr Graham the parish minister, a gentleman, scholar and *bon viveur*, who generously helps Robert Morris with books and tuition during his recuperation. His beautiful daughter Elsie is married to the Laird, and like him the Doctor falls victim to the predatory capitalist ethos. His convivial habits are worked upon until they develop into a degrading covert alcoholism, and he is eventually hounded to death by his creditors. The largest of these, and the villains of the piece, are the Crabbices, father and son. The former, beginning life as plain Peter Craib the carter, having risen into the ranks of the mercantile bourgeoisie through a mixture of graft, cunning, and ruthless self-interest, now heads the business community as a prosperous brewer and distiller. During the course of the story he is succeeded by his son Tom, who conceals his natural viciousness behind a carefully constructed façade of public respectability while systematically abusing the power that flows from his wealth. Despite a career of the most energentic depravity, he ends the story in the full flush of success, an elder of the kirk, a prominent 'philanthropist', a leading and respected public figure.

The novel's underlying framework of ideas reflects an important contemporary debate about the nature of the new industrial society and its implications for the individual and the state. Scotland had grown within a couple of generations into one of the top three or four countries in the developed world, and the figure of the distiller/brewer provided a uniquely appropriate symbol for this change. Until the rise of the Buchanans and Dewars, the so-called 'Whisky Barons', at the end of the century, distilling did not occupy a very prominent position in industrial mythology, with few figures to challenge the great ship-builders and ironmasters of popular memory. Yet brewing and distilling made up one of the biggest slices of Scottish business enterprise in the mid-Victorian period; they were highly capitalised, highly mechanised, big employers whose activities implied the whole nexus of social change involved in industrialisation and modernisation. Whisky consumption had increased enormously after the Napoleonic Wars. Within the last fifteen years there had been a fifty per cent increase in output and the figure was climbing steeply even as Alexander wrote.

But there were other reasons why his attention might be attracted to the symbolic possibilities of the drink trade. The great Edinburgh and Glasgow brewers had yet to achieve their national dominance and Aberdeen was still a flourishing brewing centre, for much of the century second only to Glasgow in the scale of output. As with whisky, beer production had been climbing steadily, more than doubling between 1850 and 1865. Drunkenness was a serious and growing problem. Until the passage of the Forbes-Mackenzie Act in 1853 which closed Scottish pubs on Sunday and shut them at eleven p.m. on other nights (at least in theory—it was widely disregarded), it was possible to drink round the clock seven days a week. Saturday was pay night and for many male Scots it marked the start of a shattering binge which went on right through Sunday—the most drunken and violent day of the week—and Monday, St Monday as it was called, because of the widespread tendency to be unfit for work until the following day. Such habits could be indulged more freely in Aberdeen than in any other city in Scotland. Reckoning only licenced premises, and disregarding shebeens and illicit dram-shops, mid-Victorian Aberdeen had one drinking-place for every 188 of its citizens. Glasgow had one per 1,000.

The right to make money by manufacturing and selling drink (or anything else for that matter), regardless of the consequences, lay at the heart of the contemporary doctrines of *laissez faire* and the free market economy. Pressure groups which urged the restriction or suppression of a major industry like the drink trade through state intervention had a key position, therefore, in the evolution of ideas about the state and its relation to the individual. The Temperance Movement was a powerful and highly organised lobby with roots going back deep into popular radicalism; it enjoyed close ties with the Liberal party in Scotland. It also had the warm support of William Alexander. Alexander does not appear to have been personally active in the movement, but he espoused its cause in the columns of his newspaper, and he makes Robert Morris, the most estimable of his characters in the *Laird of Drammoch-dyle*, president of the Strathaven Temperance Society.

Yet even here he takes an independent line. Instead of concentrating on the shortcomings of the poor as the Temperance reformers did, he turns the spotlight on the upper classes; in Strathaven it is the gentry and the educated professionals who get drunk and batter their wives. In any case, the Temperance debate provides only the immediate occasion of the story. Alexander is more interested in its theoretical implications and from them he derives the central argument of the novel which deals with the bruising encounter of his central characters with the destructive side of capitalism. He is not crudely anti-materialistic. Robert Morris rises to a well-deserved competence through his version of the business ethic, but George Ross, the innkeeper, loses everything because he is not competitive or crooked enough to thrive within a basically corrupt ethos. In Strathaven nearly everything is for sale or available through the flourishing spoils-system based on local business connections. As the engineer Jamie Monro remarks:

> in the like of Strathaven they're a' linkit thegither in bits o' cliques an' family relationships. An' fan an openin' occurs, an' some gawpus that happens to hae a fader or an uncle o' some standin', casts his ee upon't; or his mither thinks 'This wud dee richt weel wi' oor Johnny'—or his daddy is feelin' tiret o' mainteenin' the useless howffin—forthwith the strings begin to be pull't. This man can get the Baillie's lug, an' that the Shirra's—I can sair your business a gweed turn, an' maybe ye cud dee mine a bad ane; so that the hail local circle is secured; or at least a 'workin' majority'. Noo in big toons it's impossible to get the en's o' a' the strings in your ain han'. An' so merit may hae some chance. In sma' toons it has nane.

Alexander is scathing about the commercialism of the marriage market, as we see in the episode where Mrs Crabbice contrives the union of her daughter Eliza with a drunken booby old enough to be her father merely to acquire his estate. This is a common enough theme in Victorian fiction. But Alexander shows it happening at every social level, and when he marries off Robert Morris to the sensible and virtuous governess Agnes Wilson he carefully points out that marriage is an imperfect institution, and they will not live happily ever after. The ending further underlines his originality: with Robert and Agnes soberly entering a testing future, Edward Boyce a certified lunatic, his wife Elsie dead with a broken heart, Dr Graham hounded to his grave, the lawyer Daniel Lillie murdered in a ditch, George Ross sunk in swinish apathy in a backstreet dram-shop, the only character who seems destined for happiness is the abominable Tom Crabbice. Vice triumphs. And the laird and the minister, those twin pillars of the older Scotland, are swept aside and the new capitalist bourgeoisie installed in their place.

It has been customary to regard the Victorian period as a time of under-achievement and failure in Scottish writing. Critics, concentrating exclusively on a book-culture produced for the London-dominated literary market have regarded the writings of the mainly professional novelists who serviced it, the so-called Kailyard School including Sir J M Barrie, 'Ian Maclaren' (Dr John Watson), and S R Crockett with their characteristically sentimental, backward-looking rural world-picture as the authentic voice of the period. They have often gone on to condemn these writers for turning their backs upon the contemporary scene and the harsh realities of urban and industrial Scotland, seeing in their flight from reality evidence of a shameful failure of imaginative nerve. This is one of the central assumptions of recent cultural history and many subsequent judgements have been made in the light of it crucial to the Scots' perception of themselves. If it is not true, and it is not, then a fundamental revision of perspectives will have to take place. An independent Scottish literary market subsisted vigorously throughout the Victorian period, with the national press sustaining an extensive popular literature dealing freely with contemporary social conditions amongst which the novels of William Alexander have, for the most part, lain hidden for upwards of a century. He is clearly a significant novelist, and our re-assessment of him and of the movement he represents is a task of some urgency.

The Aberdeen Free Press,

PETERHEAD, FRASERBURGH, & BUCHAN NEWS

AND NORTH OF SCOTLAND ADVERTISER.

No. 2 | PRICE ONE PENNY. | AGRICULTURE, COMMERCE, LITERATURE; FREE INSTITUTIONS AND RESPONSIBLE GOVERNMENT. | TUESDAY, JUNE 27, 1865.

A NOTE ON THE SOURCE

The city edition of the *Free Press* was a typical Victorian newspaper. It was priced at 1*d.* and issued weekly on Tuesdays from the office in Concert Court off Broad Street in Aberdeen. It was printed on two large folio sheets carrying six columns to the page, amounting in all to about 40,000 words of densely compact reading matter. Except in advertisements which occupied the whole of the front page there were no illustrations, and the title was blazoned on the masthead in a mixture of gothic and bold roman type as *The Aberdeen Free Press, Peterhead, Fraserburgh, & Buchan News & North of Scotland Advertiser.*

The paper was owned by a private partnership whose business records have not survived. It is difficult, therefore, to piece together its day-to-day operations with any precision, although something can be inferred from the practice of other papers. Its permanent establishment was small. What Victorians called the 'literary department' probably comprised the editor, sub-editor, and one, or possibly two, reporters. It would have had a cashier with a couple of assistants to look after the commercial side of the business, a team of compositors who would have set the paper by hand, and a number of pressmen who would physically reproduce it, probably on a steam-driven flat-bed press. The despatch department would have had a supervisor and a number of boys employed part-time. Finally there was a jobbing department doing miscellaneous printing for the local market, everything from handbills and posters to pamphlets and books, which provided a dependable source of additional revenue. Although most of Alexander's books and pamphlets were distributed by outside publishers they were actually printed on his own presses in Concert Court.

Since competition quickly pushed the selling-price down to or below the cost of production, advertising was the life-blood of successful newspaper enterprise and a thriving paper might have as much as fifty per cent of its column-space devoted to this purpose. The *Free Press* shows a fairly typical blend, with shipping and railway company timetables, public notices, lets of salmon fishings and grazing land, notices of property, timber and ship sales, and a variety of goods and services ranging from ironmongery and second-hand machinery to black lead, soft soap, and false teeth. The leader columns could be found on pages two and three along with further advertisements and a mixture of local and general news. Many papers employed specialist leader writers, but the *Free Press* tended to rely upon its own staff, notably the editor William McCombie, and various of its proprietors including the local businessman David Macallan who had founded the paper in 1853. McCombie was a distinguished intellectual with a wide range of interests and a quite separate career as an agriculturist, in which subject he was an authority in his own right. For many years he enjoyed fairly poor health and relied on Alexander to look after the day to day running of the paper, sending in his leading articles and other copy by post from his farm in the Howe of Alford some thirty miles outside Aberdeen. The paper took its stand on land reform, voluntaryism (that is private as opposed to state endowment for churches), the abolition of hereditary privileges, and temperance reform. It was considered so radical that many established newsagents would not sell it and the paper had to work out its own distribution network using other outlets.

World news was gathered telegraphically and coverage was comprehensive but usually, because of the cost, relatively brief. Local news, on the other hand, was covered with enormous detail and particularity with long verbatim reports of council, police commission, presbytery and magistrates' meetings. In the old days, most Scots papers had got their copy from other published sources and relied on part-time correspondents for their local news. As the press revolution gathered momentum after the repeal of the Stamp Act in 1855, however, a new class of professional journalists came into being. Alexander was one of the pioneers who established by his tact and persistence, and in the teeth of official opposition, the right of access by the press to every aspect of contemporary public life. He was later created Vice-President of the Institute of Journalists in recognition of his services.

Generally speaking reporting was extremely objective and of a very high standard, and little escaped Alexander's notebook. He had a masterly ability to convey the atmosphere of public meetings, the procedural chicanery, the turmoil and commotion, the jeers, catcalls and witty asides of a political ethos noticeably more turbulent than our own. His coverage of Aberdeen ward meetings still makes memorable reading. He had a tendency, widely reflected in the Scottish press, to report what people said exactly as they said it, and if it was in Scots (and it often was) not to translate it silently into standard English. The best of his work in this way can be seen in a series of lengthy interviews he did some years later with, amongst others, the remarkable George

Webster, the leading thief-taker in the North-East, whose reminiscences published as *A Criminal Officer of the Old School* (Aberdeen 1880) are a minor masterpiece of acute characterisation and narrative skill, and in vernacular Scots throughout.

The literary section of the paper occupied part of page four alongside local reports and miscellaneous general news. In 1865 the main offering was the *Laird of Drammochdyle*, along with various pieces of local poetry (often of a good standard) and book and magazine reviews. The implications of *Drammochdyle* may have been underlined for readers by the grim contents of the column that lay alongside it during most of its run—the unfolding crisis of the great cattle plague or *rinderpest* that threatened to devastate the North-East economy during the autumn and winter of 1865–6. The disease reached Britain from eastern Europe, and hit Aberdeenshire in June 1865. Nobody living had seen it before and nobody knew how to treat it. As its appalling virulence became apparent the agricultural interest in Aberdeenshire reacted with lightning speed to form a highly organised mutual protection association with a central directory in the city and branches in every parish. A complete bureaucratic structure with its own vets and inspectors was conjured virtually out of nothing and a system of voluntary levies raised to compensate members for what quickly became a policy of slaughter at sight. The *Free Press* provided its communications system, with the editor William McCombie on the central committee, and Alexander pouring forth column upon column of up-to-the-minute reports on the situation. There was effective control of movement of cattle and a watch kept on the main southern drove routes as the county imposed upon itself a virtual state of seige. While losses mounted in the south, the situation in Aberdeenshire was held in check, and the lessons learned there had an important influence on Government strategies to contain the epidemic. The successful collective effort mounted in Aberdeenshire to combat this major threat to the local economy provides a most suggestive context for the study of destructive individualism which forms the theme of the novel, and acts as a further reminder of Alexander's imaginative responsiveness to the social realities of the Scotland of his day.

Dr William Alexander.

Reproduced by courtesy of Aberdeen Museum and Art Gallery.

THE HOUSE OF DRAMMOCHDYLE

EDWARD BOYCE, Esq. of Drammochdyle, was the only son of the late Jeremiah Boyce, a retired ornament of the legal profession, who in his prime had gone on circuit with the Lords of Session as Advocate-Depute, and at a later date, when his shade of politics was in the ascendant, had received the reward of faithful services and eminent legal attainments in the appointment to the sheriffship of a far north county of Scotland, which he visited for a few days twice every year, or at any rate once, to dispense law and justice. He was a careful man, and of the fruits of his industry and thrift had bought the estate of Drammochdyle, then in a state of considerable disrepair. This he set himself to remedy; and soon was as deep in the reclamation, drainage, and enclosure of land, as ever he had been in the intricacies of Coke-upon-Lyttleton, or the verbiage of law pleas and criminal indictments. His family consisted of his wife, one son whose name has been already mentioned, and who is the principal hero of this story, and two daughters, one of whom was dead and the other married to a wealthy 'old Indian', who lived in state somewhere nearer the sun than Drammochdyle. In his son, then, the hopes of the old lawyer, or, as his neighbours called him after he came to reside at Drammochdyle, 'the Shirra', were in a large measure centered. He trusted to make him a still more eminent and successful lawyer than he had been himself; for why he started on a vantage ground as compared with the founder of the family who had clambered upward from the position of a mere friendless apprentice boy. Young Edward knew nothing of the *res angusta domi* that

1

had hampered the early career of old Jeremiah. And after passing through the full university curriculum with fair credit he was at once put under the auspices of a first-class legal firm to prepare him for taking his place at the bar.

Meanwhile Sheriff Boyce was busy upon the improvement of his estate. The extension of his house was resolved upon, for it was not desirable or congruous that Patrick Crabbice, Esq. of Vatville, the opulent brewer and distiller of Strathaven, who owned but a mere garden plot of land in comparison, should possess a finer house than the laird of Drammochdyle. It was, moreover, requisite that the whole matter of the family inheritance should be settled on a right and stable basis; that every contingency that might endanger the permanency of the house of Boyce among the landed gentry of the district should be guarded against. And in that view, now that the soil had been pretty well improved, Jeremiah Boyce was proceeding, with the greatest possible professional relish, toward getting completed a deed of entail, which should bind the lands to his family and their descendants in all time coming, when an event occurred that laid an emphatic arrest upon his plans. This was his own death. A contingency which, be it said, the old lawyer, like some few others, had rather overlooked in the midst of his schemes. Albeit it had not come prematurely, for he was several years beyond the limit of three score and ten.

Our desultory story opens some twelve months after this date.

Chapter I

TWO WAYFARERS

'An' ye dinna think the lot o' a workin' man a hard ane Bob? Ye dinna think it a hard fate to be condemned to toil on for ten hours a-day, a' the year roun', for a bare guinea a-week; an' broken time no' countit; an' wi' no prospect o' ever gettin' your head heicher in this warld?'

'Weel I canna' say I do, Geordie. But, in the first place, I hardly think ye've stated the case fairly. Grantit the ten hours o' daily toil, a man micht hae much greater reason to compleen, as lang as he has health an' strength for 't; but it 's drivin' the nail owre hard to say that even *we* have nae chance o' ever gettin' abeen that if we choose.'

'Aye hopefu' Bobbie. Whan we get abeen't it'll be under the reef o' the poor-house I expect, or how else tell me? Here noo is our maister—to start a business like his requires, I've been tauld, a lang way ayont a thousan' pounds. Will you or mysel' ever possess a fourth part o' that sum?'

'Likely aneuch no. Yet, wi' common sense to guide us, an' the twa common-place virtues o' steadiness an' sobriety, we may be able to clim' the brae a wee bit in some shape, or at the warst meet the hardships o' our obscure fate manfully.'

'Weel as for that I suppose we've baith a fair share o' common sense; and nane o's are muckle gi'en to spreein'; but I dinna see that that adds muckle to our yearly income.'

'No, but, Geordie, ye forget—'

'Oh, aye—ye speak o' sobriety. I suppose, that means to join the teetotal, to forswear gweed liquor—although ye had no better

3

reason than just because ye're owre scrubby to pay for't—an' hain the bawbees that gang for that, an' tobacco or snuff.'

'No, Geordie; sobriety means a good deal mair than that. Though takin't in your ain narrow sense, I canna see hoo a workin' man could be justified in spendin' so much o's money upon strong drink as owre mony o' us do. If the money spent on drink—and if ye like tobacco or snuff—were saved, it, by itsel', would in mony a case make a' the difference atween an auld age o' misery, and ane o' comfort. But as I was sayin', ye forgot hoo mony that hae nae better inheritance in life than oursels in this respect, yet, by steady conduct, an' intelligent use o' sic faculties as they hae, against whatever difficulties or discouragements they may meet, fill usefu' an' respectable positions in the warld. An' the great mass o' mankin' can expect nae mair. Its only the exceptionally talented, or the exceptionally fortunate that need hope for greater things.'

'I tell ye, Bob, it's nae use; there's just twa ways for a workin' man to better himsel'—marry a wife wi' a tocher; or emigrate to some place where labour comman's something like a proper reward—where the workin' man's in as much repute as his maister, in place o' being obleeged, as Robbie Burns has it—

> To beg a brother of the earth
> To give him leave to toil.'

The interlocutors were a couple of young men in the guise of working joiners, or house carpenters. Each had his basket of tools slung over his shoulder; and as they trudged along side by side they had taken to discussing their prospects in life. It was a raw autumn morning, and the young ice formed on the small pools in the horses' hoofmarks cracked loudly under their feet as they tramped along the rough country road, which led over a pretty wide common into the turnpike of more civilised aspect, that ran between the country town of Strathaven, and the far interior whither pedlars and beggars trudged a-foot, to ply their respective vocations among the simple minded rustics; and whither sportsmen from the sunnier southward were wont to migrate at the proper season, per the Tallyho stage coach, to shoot hares and grouse. The elder of the two, George Ross, could be very little, if at all, over twenty-five, and his companion, Robert Morris, was a year or two younger. George was a rather handsome athletic fellow of fair complexion and ruddy hue; and it was this physical advantage, together with the fact that he had had some three years longer experience of journeyman life than Robert Morris, that made him at times assume an air of something like superiority over his old playmate and school companion, who was of slighter frame, and, so far as *physique* went, altogether less fitted to attract favourable notice, though the attentive observer might have discovered in his pale, almost sallow face and dark grey eyes, traces of greater thoughtfulness and intelligence than in the case of his friend and fellow workman.

'Weel, Geordie,' continued Robert Morris, 'I micht seek to better my position in life by emigration; but by marryin' a wife wi' money—never!'

'Aha, Bob,' laughed George Ross, 'Wait till ye've got the chance afore ye quarrel wi't.'

'No; its true aneuch I'm little likely ever to hae the chance; but, as a matter o' principle, I would refuse it though I had. Why, man, the very fact o' your wife haein' command o' the purse—even though she were an amiable woman—would put you in a humiliated condition as head o' the house. An' if she were en-dowed wi' some o' the less lovable qualities o' even a woman's nature, it's likely she would take occasion to let you feel your humiliation.'

'I'll take the risk Bob,' continued George Ross, 'An' if ye had a little mair experience o' what it is to fight your ain way in the warld, I've nae doot but some of your fine notions on sic-like subjects 'ill sober doon a bit.'

'No, no, Geordie, I think they're mair sobered doon than your ain even; they'll dee weel aneuch for every day wear,' was the reply.

By this time our pedestrian friends had reached the lee side of a pretty long range of plantation that skirted the road, and lent its friendly shelter from the cutting north-east wind. A little way on there was a two leaved green gate, with the customary side wickets and porter's lodge, indicating that if one wished to see 'the laird', here was the point at which his steps must diverge from the king's highway. They opened one of the wickets, for the porter or porteress appeared to be not yet astir, and proceeded up the broad gravelled carriageway, bordered by laurel and other evergreen shrubs and trees, that wound onward to the mansion house of Drammochdyle.

'What say ye than, Bobbie,' resumed George Ross, 'to the possession o' an estate like this o' Drammochdyle, o' which our auld skweel companion, Ned Boyce, is noo owner? Ye would hae some scruples o' conscience against acceptin' that tee nae doot?'

'Not if it cam by fair and honest means.'

'Oh; an' ye admit than that it's better to be a laird than a workin' man?'

'In some respects it may be.'

'Some respects. Come noo, Bob, dinna draw it owre strong upo' me. Say honestly, man, wudna ye raither be in the place o' the young laird o' Drammochdyle—the owner o' a' these fertile acres—than be only Bob Morris the widow's son whase wardly possessions consist o' his kit o' tools an' the claes he stan's in?'

'I'm no prepared to say that I would, Geordie.'

'No prepared to say that ye would—ye're a rare philosopher, Bob! Hoo no prepared?'

'As Bob Morris the widow's son I ken my ain burden, an' feel that if it be at times heavy aneuch yet my back can bear't. As laird o' Drammochdyle I neither ken the burden, nor could venture to say if I should be able to bear't.'

'Aye, aye, Bob, I suppose ye mean to say ye might fail to do your duty in that position?'

'I micht, an' its likely aneuch I should.'

'Weel there may be something in that. But suppose ye did fail ye would only be like ither lairds. They're a meeserable set the haill lot o' them for that maitter. They care for little but to grind the noses o' the poor for their ain advantage. But then if ye were in young Drammochdyle's place noo, would ye not, in your ain way o' thinkin', hae a far better startin' point for what I suppose ye would ca' ''a usefu' career'' in life, no to speak o' what only the like o' me, of coorse, would think o'—that is haein' a far mair desirable means o' livelihood for yoursel?'

'Life's before us baith,' replied Robert Morris thoughtfully, 'an' I dinna doot but his position has difficulties, an' temptations aneuch to try the man that's in't. But grant me health an' strength to dee my pairt, an' I'll no envy him nor ony ither man.'

The conversation ceased. They had now reached the mansion-house of Drammochdyle, pleasantly situated on a southward-sloping lawn, dotted over with hard-wood trees. Upon this house their employer, Mr. Barkus, master builder in Strathaven, was engaged; for a new wing was being added to the older portion of it which dated from the close of the sixteenth century, to make the accommodation more complete, and convert the whole into a somewhat imposing, if slightly incongruous, pile, understood to be of the Elizabethan order of architecture.

Chapter II

THE OLD LAIRD AND THE YOUNG ONE

IF a sentence or two in the way of moralising be permissible in this veracious chronicle, we feel it to be due on our part toward the memory of the personage first introduced to our readers.

Jeremiah Boyce, 'the Shirra', was the man who of all others bulked most largely in our youthful imagination. Physically, with his long stately stride, his arms crossed behind his back, his shaggy grey head, and his jolly red nose, he commanded a respect not unmingled with something like awe. But that was not all; he was a shrewd, experienced man of business, and could give sound advice on most things; and, albeit, he had a temper of his own, was not indisposed to give it—and with painstaking attention when occasion required—to his humbler neighbours, by one of whom his character was summed up in the comprehensive statement that he was 'their Gweed an' their deil tee'. From whose ominous approach have we slunk away so stealthily, from whom have we received more stern reproofs? Was it not in *his* water that we first in a surreptitious manner practised the 'gentle art' by angling for minnows with a bent pin, and dodging under the bank with an old wicker creel, and then 'setting lines' in front of his very mansion; and when we had advanced the length of a patched up rod and flies, who, to our horror, should we meet as we returned home but the Shirra, who demanded to know what we had got in that bag? And after inspecting the half-dozen diminutive trouts stored therein, actually pulled a couple of shillings from his green silk purse, and put them in our trembling hand under our incredulous eyes to buy a new line and hooks!

Aye peace, profound peace to his memory. With all his irascibility, and all those out-bursts of temper—notwithstanding that he threatened to have us punished with the rigour of the law as an incorrigible poacher, who killed his salmon smolts, and shot his hares, who was it but the Shirra, who in days not long after on meeting us, an obscure and unknown item in the city population, took us to his hotel to inquire of our prospects, spoke a few encouraging words in his own abrupt way, and at parting— we hardly knew how—left in our fist a veritable gold sovereign, the first we ever possessed.

But the Shirra had departed this life; and, we conclude, will be little better or worse of these remarks. Let us speak of his son.

Edward Boyce had engaged in the study of the law, quite as much to satisfy his father's wish as from any enthusiastic attachment to it on his own part; and accordingly as he had, since his father's decease, passed his examinations, and been admitted to the bar, it was no very long time ere he resolved upon, at least, a temporary abandonment of professional pursuits, in order that he might devote himself to the management of his estate; which, as it now yielded a clear rental of some £700 a-year, seemed pretty nearly sufficient for his wants. By this course, he could, meanwhile gratify his taste for country pursuits, and as it were, 'live among his own people', by whom the young man was universally known and very generally liked. And then, should occasion call for it, he could resume professional practice hereafter.

Almost the only part of his father's plans in connexion with the estate of Drammochdyle that had been left uncompleted, were the rehabilitation of the mansion house and the carrying out of the entail. The latter of these Edward Boyce did not regard as by any means so pressing, as it had seemed to the old Shirra to be; the former he set himself to finish in accordance with the arrangements made before his father's death. And it was while engaged in discussing some of the details of the work with Mr. Barkus, the builder, in front of the house, only a few days after the date of the conversation, recorded in our second chapter, that the two were startled by the crash of breaking planks and falling material, accompanied by the hasty and excited exclamations of some of the workmen engaged upon the wing in course of erection. On hurrying to the spot it was seen that a scaffolding at a considerable elevation had given way, from some unknown cause, precipitating several workmen who were upon it, from a height of some twenty feet to the ground, amid a heap of broken wood and other debris. Among those who had been thrown down were George Ross and Robert Morris. The former it was quickly seen had escaped with comparatively little injury; as had also the other workmen with the exception of Robert Morris, upon whom the weight of almost the whole mass had fallen. On being extricated with some difficulty, his wounds were found to be of a very severe character. Besides a deep gash in his cheek, one of his hands was much injured by twisting, and his left leg evidently fractured below the knee. The unfortunate young man was carried round to the servants' Hall, and a messenger despatched on horseback to Strathaven, for the doctor who soon arrived. On examining the fractured limb, Dr. Milner merely uttered the words 'poor fellow', and soon thereafter took occasion to retire to another room, along with Edward Boyce and Mr. Barkus. When there he at once, after uttering certain strong expletives anent the carelessness of builders in general in looking to the safety of their workmen, and a significant glance at Mr. Barkus, informed them that the fracture was one of a very bad kind, while the ankle joint had also been so seriously injured as, he believed, to leave no resort save amputation.

'Unfortunate laddie', exclaimed Mr. Barkus, too much absorbed in the calamity to make any personal application, 'What in the world will become o' him? He is the only support of his widowed mither and sister.'

'He and they must and shall be cared for', was the warmly-expressed reply of Edward Boyce, who had not forgot the playmate of his boyish days, though the lapse of time, and difference in social position, which comes to be more recognised as youths develope into young men, had put some considerable measure of restraint on their intercourse at such times as they had casually met for a few years past.

'Well, gentlemen', said the Doctor, 'we needn't discuss the point meanwhile. There's a Providence above him and us too'.

'Nae doot', doctor, 'nae doot; but the lad's a lamiter for life, ye say; he'll never be fit for his occupation again', answered Mr. Barkus.

'Tut, man, as if there weren't better, as well as safer occupations than climbing your ricketty scaffolding. I brought a few things with me, Mr. Boyce, and we'll go and do what temporary bandaging we need meantime. Will ye go over and tell the poor laddie's mither, Barkus, for the story will soon get wings, and feet too, as it goes, and don't say too much to alarm her, mind ye.'

Robert Morris had not been unobservant of Dr. Milner's movements, nor oblivious to their signification; and accordingly when the worthy practitioner, who under a somewhat rough exterior carried a really humane and tender heart, as well as a light and skilful hand, again entered the hall, he relieved any embarrassment on his part by requesting to be at once told the worst. The request was made in a way that indicated a mind prepared calmly to hear the reply, and firmly yet kindly the inevitable consequence of the accident was told by the doctor.

Chapter III

THE LOST LIMB

'It's only to lose a limb!' Ah well; when the staggering realization of that comes first home in all its force to the heart of a young man, who but of yesterday, or it may be but an hour ago, was buoyant with hope; full of glowing pictures of, and dazzling schemes for, the future, as beseems the spring-time of life, who may picture the terrible shock! Maimed, crippled, hopelessly debarred from one half of what makes existence a blessing, in respect alike of the work and the reward; finding, now and again, that where you thought you had at least a claim to respectful pity, your plight has awakened a feeling marvellously akin to contempt; with a man's sympathies, feelings, and aspirations within your breast whole and unimpaired; yet crushed down by the withering thought that the field of a man's exertions you can enter no more, upon equal terms with others. To the sanguine mind of youth difficulties and dangers may be—indeed, in their due measure, ought to be—only the spur to exertion; but to know that you are suddenly and irremediably shorn of a part of the power—nay, of the very being—which God had given you; and that henceforth your life is of stern necessity subject to exceptional material conditions—*that* is what must needs awaken thoughts so solitary and saddening, as none may describe. And in the case of those whose means of living depend upon physical labour alone, and whose cherished hopes for the future of life have all been in the direction of free and active enterprise, the prospect that presents itself is all the more gloomy and desolate; inasmuch as the calamity seems at once to shut the avenues of honourable industry, and relegate the individual to the ranks of helpless dependance or degrading pauperism.

We know not how far such thoughts may have passed through the mind of Robert Morris, when in addition to the acute physical suffering from his broken and bruised limb, he had learned the inevitable issue of the chief injury he had received. But he bore up with the spirit of a man; and in reply to the proffers of Edward Boyce, to have him put in a comfortable room in the mansion-house, where he might lie till his recovery, his respectful but decided answer was, 'Thanks, Mr. Boyce; but I've a hame and a mither. Let me be carried hame; my comrades will carry me.'

'Yes,' said the doctor, 'I know his mother; he can be better nowhere than with her. The lads will carry him home carefully, and I will ride past for my instruments, and bring Dr. Johnston with me to assist.'

So Robert had his wish; and in that poor widow's cottage that foot was amputated, the right foot of him on whose daily labour the humble household were day by day dependent for bread.

Chapter IV

THE KIRKTOWN AND ITS INHABITANTS

Strathaven as the county town of its particular shire, was an important enough place in its own way; yet, in some respects it stood in a secondary position. It had pleased the wise forefathers of the locality to build the parish church, not where Strathaven now stood, but away on a small elevated table land, half a mile from the sea, and with a sort of mild and homely ravine curving round its north side, that forbade ready through communication that way. And the parish they had named, not Strathaven, but Dalweary. In days long gone by, when Strathaven was a mere group of a dozen fisherman's huts, its inhabitants on a Sunday morning would wind their way slowly up the valley to meet, and be lost in, the converging streams of landward people, as they gathered toward the Church, to the pleasant ting-tangling of the sedate old bell, which turned on its pivots with a hurtle, that was very audible from the spot where the industrious bellman stood, tugging away at the end of his rope, till the parson had walked gravely up the pathway, and disappeared from his view, at the opposite end of the Kirk, as he swayed round the corner to catch the proper moment of heaving the bell rope on to its hook in the wall, and marching in to the sacred edifice to see his reverence duly seated, close the pulpit door, adjust the window blind to the proper degree of shade, and then ensconce himself in the corner of the enclosed four square seat, which the rustics were wont, not too reverently, to call 'the pumphel', figuring thereby, as the enlighted reader will know, a summer enclosure for flocks and herds. And so now, when Strathaven could boast of eight to ten thousand inhabitants, the like legal provision for public worship continued, and no other. The people had still to walk out of town to their parish Church; only that the existence of one of those anomalous edifices, known as 'chapels of Ease', and several dissenting places of worship, within the borders of Strathaven, gave a sort of choice to those whose principles admitted of their either altogether deserting a venerable national institution, or hanging on to it under a mild form of ecclesiastical degradation.

The Kirktown of Dalweary, once—(if history and tradition err not)—superior to Strathaven in point of population, even, as it still was in point of ecclesiastical dignity, consisted of not quite a score of houses. Among its inhabitants were the smith, the shoe-maker, the tailor, the beadle, or bellman—Johnny Duncan to wit—the midwife, or say howdy, Mrs. Muggart—and sundry others of less note, amongst whom was the mother of Robert Morris.

Such a place as the Kirktown naturally has its own peculiar idiosyncracy. There each man knows his fellow, and every woman is well versed in the public and personal history of the whole community. And thus it happened that when Robert Morris's misfortune came upon him, he and his affairs became the topic of current interest. The beadle, just mentioned, who professed to have been bred a tailor, but who had never achieved great success in the pursuit of that useful, though not very robust calling—whose capacity as a 'tradesman' was indicated by a pro-fessional brother in the phrase, 'Why, Sir, he couldn't shape a pair of pockets for your britches properly'—the beadle—neces-sarily a person of some note in the place—as one of the leaders in questions of social as well as political interest—took up the subject at large. In virtue of his official relation to the parish minister, Dr. Graham—of whom more anon—he had been sent to make special inquiries of the doctor about his patient—Mrs. Morris and her family being dissenters, Dr. Graham had not been in the practice of calling upon them, though he felt it now to be his duty, at least, to inquire after the condition of Robert.

'The lad's dyin',' was the oracular utterance of Johnny Duncan to the pitiful women, as they gathered about him on his way back from Dr. Milner's.

'Deein'! Eh, sirs, fat *wull* come o's peer mither,' exclaimed Mrs. Ellison, the sutor's wife.

'Fat'll come o'er?' answered Johnny sharply. 'It may be the providence o' Gweed to tak 'im oot o' this warl'; for ye may weel see 't he cud never be onything else nor a peer supplicant.'

'Oh, John, dinna speak that gate; the bit an' the sup's aye gien as lang's we need it, an' life's sweet ye ken.'

'Weel weel; its nae like 't he'll store the kin lang at ony rate. But fat cud the peer stock dee supposin' he war to cour a' this? Get an' aul' horse an' ca' fish? It's no 's gin he war like oorsell wi' a trade at's finger en's 't depen's as muckle upo' gweed mental poo'ers, as the eese o' mere physical, or breet strength.'

This last magnificent sentence completely floored poor Mrs. Ellison, as Johnny meant it should; and he walked on with an air of much satisfaction, and not indisposed for the chance of astonishing some other goodwife; for Johnny was one of those individuals who, although you can never surprise them with an announcement, however startling, and who 'scorn to shaw' that your earliest intelligence of any event is fresh to them, do dearly love to flash astounding announcements upon others in the most abrupt and emphatic manner. The doctor's reply had been that Robert Morris had borne the operation well, but was very weak, and suffering much, and Johnny had deemed it a safe vaticination to transmute this intelligence as above, in dealing with the general public. To the minister, he said—'Weel, he's verra, verra wake, Sir—though he steed it oot nae that ill. But I doot the doctor has little howp o' 'im,' which was, after all, a very tolerable paraphrase of the statement actually given to him.

On the weary time that Robert Morris spent in illness and suffering, 'tis needless to dwell. How from his lesser injuries he suffered more by far than from the chief one; how when half convalescent, his anxiety to do *something*, led him to over-exert himself at some trifling pieces of work; and how, as a consequence, he paid the penalty in many long months of pain by day, and greater pain by night, till worn and aged in look, and nervously excitable as an old wife, the power to bend his mind to anything like sustained effort, in any direction whatever, was well nigh gone; and, as a desperate resource, the sketching of absurd caricatures, and the construction of doggrel verse of a grimly humourous cast, were taken to as a relief from heavier thoughts, and protection against that style of complaining and whining about personal suffering or misfortune, which is certain very quickly to make him who indulges therein a nuisance to all about him.

And certainly this is something, if it be not even a great deal; for if the patience and sympathy of our fellows, as a whole, be just sufficient to make them tolerate, and be on complacent terms with us when they see suffering borne with real patience, we may be very certain that our querulousness, even under the pressure of pain and anguish, is a dead mistake, inasmuch as in place of securing that greater commiseration which we deem ourselves entitled to, it begets a feeling of irritation that makes us be looked upon with positive aversion. A fact this that ailing people and invalids might do worse than ponder.

Chapter V

AN EVENING PARTY AT VATVILLE

The evening parties at Vatville were got up regardless of expense, and with a supreme desire to secure elegance and effect. Mr. Crabbice, the proprietor, was one of the most opulent and influential men that Strathaven could boast among its ten thousand inhabitants. Of this fact, it must be allowed, Mr. Crabbice himself was not altogether unaware, and accordingly, when the day's business was over, he chose to drive out at night to his pleasant suburban residence at Vatville, in his own handsome vehicle, with his own servant on the coach-box, in a smartish semi-livery sort of dress. He liked to keep up a befitting state. And in this he was warmly supported by the female members of his household—'Mrs. Crabbice and the Misses Crabbices'. Until Sheriff Boyce came to live in their vicinity, indeed, it was with some difficulty the Crabbices found fit 'society'. True, there was the Rev. Dr. Graham, the parish clergyman, 'a gentleman and a scholard', as Mrs. Crabbice phrased it, and his daughter Elsie. And Dr. Graham was a desirable and welcome guest at all times at Vatville. But this resulted mainly from his official position and his personal character. For at such entertainments as Patrick Crabbice, Esq., and his family loved to give, where, along with a good deal of stately ceremony and buckram display, there invariably occurred a convenient interregnum during which the gentlemen zealously devoted themselves to testing the contents of their host's cellar, set forth in liberal, and perhaps somewhat ostentatious profusion, it was felt to be a decided advantage, and even no slight comfort, to have the proceedings sanctioned by the presence of the spiritual guide of the company; and especially, when, as in the case of Dr. Graham, he was a man of a convivial turn, and possessed of a goodly share of wit and humour. And then the other residents in the neighbourhood were, with one or two exceptions, decidedly below par. Now it may be all very well to go on dazzling obscure people with the splendour of your house and equipages, as the Crabbices did among the choice of the better-to-do shopkeepers and tradesfolk of Strathaven; but even this has its limits. And ambition in this line points also at somebody to cope with, as well as some family of unquestioned standing to sidle up to as equals.

Therefore, it was that the first party at Vatville, to which Edward Boyce had been asked since his father's death, was got up with the utmost elaboration. And when the guests had assembled, and the stately procession marched toward the dining-room, it was Edward who had the honour of leading the hostess thither. How it had been contrived that he should supplant Dr. Graham, on whom that distinguished duty usually fell, we need not enquire. It was, indeed, said that Mrs. Crabbice who was a far seeing woman, had certain schemes in respect of her family, and that among these was included the project of securing Edward Boyce as a son-in-law, through the medium of her eldest daughter Eliza, a rosy beauty, who now hung gracefully on Dr. Graham's arm; while she did not very severely frown on the idea of her eldest son Tom, wooing and winning Elsie Graham, a pretty girl of eighteen, with blue eyes and flaxen curls, whom Tom was leading in to the dining-room with becoming gallantry.

It is needless to describe all the members of the company; and still more needless to detail the progress of the dinner, served by a waiter hired for the day, in addition to Mr. Crabbice's own male servant—coachman, butler, footman, as he was poor fellow. Suffice it that the most noticeable person 'amongst those present', as newspaper reporters say, and who has not been hitherto spoken of, was Benjamin Ryrie, a stout purple faced, and rather taciturn man, reputedly very wealthy, a bachelor, a county magistrate, and close friend of Mr. Crabbice, senior, in virtue probably of his admiration of and unfailing adherence to that gentlemen's opinions, especially as given from the Bench, when the worthy brewer figured thereon as one of 'Her Majesty's Justices of the Peace'. It may also be said, that the ladies retired at the proper time, and the elder gentlemen, as usual, took to discussing politics and swallowing port; in the latter of which branches they were followed with sufficient *sang froid* by the host's promising son, Mr. Tom Crabbice.

It was under such circumstances that Mr. Crabbice, senior, shone, or fancied he did. He was a shrewd man, and had seen the two sides of various things. In respect of his pecuniary position, he was what is understood by the phrase 'a self-made man'. Indeed, some who professed to know averred that not only was his father an humble itinerant dealer in butter, eggs, and small groceries, but that he even was known 'in that his day' by a less sounding patronymic than his portly rubicund-visaged son now rejoiced in. Daniel Lillie, a debauched broken down limb of the law, who at one time served as Mr. Crabbice's convenient instrument—as may hereafter appear—and next time would scandalise that worthy man by the impudent familiarities of his unruly tongue, had been known to declare to his cronies in their cups that he could recollect, as a boy, seeing the small and badly lettered deal signboard that distinguished the hovel in Strathaven of old, where the father of 'Patrick Crabbice, Esq.', dwelt, and whence he issued on his weekly rounds with his old white 'shalt' and cart, and that signboard, he averred, bore merely these words, in this order:

'PETER CRAIB,
CADGER'

Moreover, Lillie confidently asserted that the son had been christened by the same name and surname as the sire, and that when his fortunes began to rise he had expanded 'Peter Craib', and made of it the more euphonious 'Patrick Crabbice', as also that certain near relatives of less refined tastes, in this matter, for their adherence to the old surname, and their incorrigible poverty, were by him disowned. But then Lillie was no great authority, perhaps, on this or any other point. And, at any rate, why should not Mr. Crabbice have liberty to manipulate his name, according as his circumstances required, as well as other people, either by lengthening the two words of which it was composed, or sticking in a few more savouring of things heraldic, or sentimental, in the middle?

However that may be, Mr. Crabbice, at the social gatherings

under his own roof, was wont to launch forth into short, sententious speeches, from the drift of which one was led to infer that his intimacy with the leading families of the county was by no means of yesterday. He would tell you of the father of this gentleman or the uncle of that, adding, 'Ah, I knew him well; we were young together; the family has long held a good position. He was put on the commission of the Peace when I was.' It was a favourite word of his, this 'family' sounded through his nose a good deal and with an application chiefly to the 'landed gentry'. And again, this opulent trader and enlightened magistrate would descant upon the character and claims of 'the lower orders' of society with an emphatic readiness and precision that excited the utmost admiration in Benjamin Ryrie, for along with his position as a landowner, a business man, and a Justice of the Peace, he had a character to maintain as a philanthropist. And it might be Dr. Graham's knowledge of this that now prompted that rev. gentleman, after his host had pretty well expended himself in talk, to say—'Crabbice, have you any opening in your establishment for a steady, intelligent young man in the capacity of a clerk?'

'None in the meantime, Dr.,' was the reply.

'Are you likely to have by and bye?'

Well, really you see, Dr., my people very seldom leave me. Is it a meritorious case?'

'Decidedly it is; as your neighbour, young Boyce, could have told you, had he not thought fit to desert our company.' (Edward Boyce had left the elderly gentlemen a little before, along with his companion, Tom Crabbice, whom he had persuaded to give a somewhat reluctant consent to joining the ladies.) 'It is a fine young fellow,' continued Dr. Graham, 'who got badly lamed at the erection of his newly finished house.'

'Ah, so; I heard him speak of the lad's accident. And he said he would do something for him in consequence.'

'Yes, yes; Boyce would gladly give him money, but that's not the thing. Robert Morris is too independent in spirit to accept the dole of charity.'

'Quite right. I like to see that spirit—it is now almost extinct among the lower classes of society—pass the wine, Dr.'

'What he wants is some honest employment, at which he could earn his bread and support his mother and sister by his own exertions.'

'Aye; let me see. His mother—she's an active woman, per-haps? Any sisters did you say?'

'Yes; one young sister.'

'Very good. Pity to break up such a nice family. Well; and Mr. Boyce thinks he could trust him with an advance of money?'

'He knows he could trust him though it were thousands.'

'Aye; very good; very good—we need trustworthy people now-a-days; and the sister is a good-looking, smart girl?'

'A pretty and intelligent girl, I believe. Elsie could tell you better about that.'

'Doctor,' ejaculated Mr. Crabbice emphatically, stretching himself backward on his chair and speaking deliberately, 'doctor, an idea strikes me. I can do something better for that young man than make him a mere clerk, with £40 or £50 a-year which, you know, is the current rate for an efficient man in Strathaven. You know the Mill Inn?'

'I should think I do, Crabbice.'

'It's a capital property that, or ought to be. Fine accommo-dation in the house, superior stables, and other offices. Well, I have been on the outlook for a good tenant these several weeks. That wretched fellow, Jack Adams, who leased it but a couple of years ago, has got so muddled with drink that everything has gone to wrack and ruin; and the tenant before him I was obliged to poind and sequestrate. Oh it's more than mortal man could tell, the trouble of mind one has with these incapable and unprin-cipled people, not to speak of pecuniary loss.'

'Vera true,' interposed Mr. Ryrie—or 'the Captain', as he was usually called, in virtue of his having at one time held a com-mission in the county militia—this being about the period of the evening when that gentleman got mellowed sufficiently to con-verse freely.

'Now, Dr.,' continued Mr. Crabbice, it strikes me that if this young man Morris is thoroughly steady, if his mother is an active woman, and his sister a smart, tidy girl, and if he stands, as you say he does, with Mr. Boyce—such an opening rarely occurs.'

'Such an opening as what?'

'Why, I'm to advertise the Mill Inn; and I've no doubt, I'll have scores of candidates; but I pledge you my word o' honour, Dr. I'll give the preference to this young man as a tenant, upon your recommendation; and with the security of Mr. Boyce's name.'

'Capital Vatville—a vera leeberal offer,' said Captain Ryrie, draining his glass, 'capital'.

'I always like to encourage well doing young men; though many's the one I've assisted into business, who has made me a very black return,' pursued Mr. Crabbice.

'Nae doot o't' said Captain Ryrie.

'I doubt very much,' replied Dr. Graham, speaking with thoughtful deliberation, 'I doubt very much if your scheme will do; the lad has no money at any rate; and it needs cash to become an inn-keeper.'

'Or credit; you say Mr. Boyce would do something that way for him.'

'Well, no doubt, yet'—and Dr. Graham hesitated still more— 'I doubt if he would accept your offer.'

'Ah—not exactly an offer, Dr. But I say I'll prefer him as a tenant. No, I don't need to offer to any individual, when scores will be seeking it.'

'Be it so; but I sha'nt be surprised if he were to refuse to become tenant of an inn under any conditions.'

'Oh, indeed—as how?'

'Upon conscientious grounds.'

'Con-scien-tious!' muttered Captain Ryrie in a bewildered way.

'Yes; he abstains altogether from strong drink himself upon principle. And I should'nt wonder if he refuse to have anything to do with selling it to other people.'

'Well, Dr.,' answered Mr. Crabbice in a severe and almost haughty tone, 'I've seen a good deal of ingratitude among the lower orders; but, if the young man chooses to kick at his bread and butter in that way, I say he deserves to be left to his fate; that's all.'

'Cap-ital, Vatville,' ejaculated Captain Ryrie, 'pon my word— refuse a respectable way o' doin'—a beg-gar to choose—Yes, thank ye, I'll tak a glass o' the claret now.'

'And suppose you leave him to his fate, Crabbice,' said Dr. Graham, with some animation, 'It's but leaving the lad to face poverty with a clear conscience. And, under the circumstances, even that phantom might not be so terrible. With poverty, I presume, he is on pretty familiar terms; and seems to have managed to rub on rather smoothly with the gaunt dame, whose very visage terrifies so many soft-hearted people, and drives certain of them into ugly sloughs, rather than they will honestly shake hands with her. And those of "the lower orders", even, my excellent friend, who adopt the unsafe habit of thinking for themselves, are sometimes unmanageable in a troublesome degree, when they take their stand upon what they call principle. It is not, however, that I have any sympathy with his notions, observe you. Yet, I suspect he will be rather a stickler on these points. But after all the scheme may be tried.'

A call to join the ladies put an end to the conversation for a time. After coffee, the propriety of making Robert Morris tenant of the Mill Inn was again talked over, and warmly supported by Edward Boyce, who over-ruled Dr. Graham's doubts as to Robert's conscientious objections, while Tom Crabbice laughed loudly at the idea of any such consideration preventing the lamed joiner availing himself of such a chance of bettering his fortune.

Chapter VI

THE CRABBICE FAMILY AT HOME

'Mamma, don't you think Elsie Graham was very bold and forward with the young gentlemen last night?' said Eliza Crabbice to her mother, on the day after the 'party' described in the last chapter. The lady of Vatville, it may be proper to state, was seated in the parlour with her daughters for a little quiet chat, while they waited the return of Messrs. Crabbice, senior, and junior, to dinner.

'Yes, Mamma,' broke in Maria, the second daughter of the house, somewhat wickedly, 'because *she* happened to receive the attentions of Edward Boyce in place of our Eliza.'

'Maria, you naughty girl, I'm sure that's not what I meant,' returned Miss Eliza, angrily. 'Didn't you observe, Mamma, that she was very saucy with our own Tom?'

'I did, indeed, my dear; and it's very wrong of you, Maria, to speak that way to your sister; and that it is. I think our Tom has a right to get better treatment from the likes o' Elsie Graham now—and that he has.'

'I daresay, Tom won't break his heart about it,' muttered the incorrigible Maria.

'And she *was* too forward with Mr. Boyce,' continued Mrs. Crabbice. 'It's not becoming the likes of her, at any rate, to be so familiar with a man of Mr. Boyce's position. I'm sure *you* wouldn't have been so forward, Eliza.'

'She hadn't the chance, just,' again muttered Maria, *sotto voce*, as she crossed the room for a piece of crochet work.

And probably this was not very far from the truth. For the

attentions shown by Edward Boyce to Miss Graham on the preceding evening, were, without question, too assiduous to admit of Miss Crabbice, or any other young lady in the company, presenting her attractions to him with any fair chance of their being rightly appreciated. To Mrs. Crabbice, whose little scheme in this relation we have briefly indicated, the fact was in every sense mortifying; and it was little less so to Miss Crabbice, who had shown no unwillingness to do her part in the carrying out of the scheme. What the consequences might be no one could well predict. Hitherto the Crabbices had lived on intimate and highly friendly terms with Dr. and Miss Graham; but the fact now forced itself very strongly upon Mrs Crabbice's mind, that Eliza Graham, in point of position, was by no means the equal of her own daughters. And perhaps her own well meant kindness in accepting Miss Graham on an equal footing with her own family, was leading the foolish girl into assumptions unbecoming her station, as a mere presbyterian clergyman's daughter. Must she not really—in the exercise of a motherly vigilance—warn her as to the needful amount of reserve in receiving the off-hand compliments of a man with such prospects as those of Mr. Boyce? Mrs. Crabbice thought so; and the question of an unfulfilled duty in this particular began to lie heavy on her conscience.

'And besides,' pursued Miss Crabbice, 'Peggy Brown, our housemaid, told me that Edward Boyce has met Elsie Graham often and often at the widow Morris's, and walked home with her. Peggy told me that this very day.'

'How shocking!' exlaimed Mrs. Crabbice, elevating her hands.

'Yes, and Peggy told me that Mrs. Ellison told her that they walked together all the way to the manse, arm in arm, after it was evening. For Johnnie Duncan, the beadle, saw them standing together at the manse gate ever so long, when it was quite dark.'

'Well, well!' said the judicious matron, with a doleful shake of the head, 'the unhappy girl has wanted a mother's training to be sure; and that she has.'

'And what right had Elsie Graham to go to the Morris's at all, when they're dissenters, and don't go to the church?'

'And you may say it, my dear; for I've heared tell that the young man, Robert Morris, though he is no better nor a cripple and a pauper, and a mendicant, is very ondependent, and has very sceptic and unbecoming opinions for one of his class; and that he has.'

'He is a teetotaller, mamma,' said Maria. 'Isn't that very wrong—papa would say so, I'm sure; only he wants him to be tenant of the Mill Inn.'

'Don't scandalize your own father now, Maria,' exclaimed Mrs. Crabbice, with emphasis, 'for the sake of people who may be proud to look up to him.'

The entrance of papa at this very point interrupted the conversation however.

Mr. Crabbice was not talkative in his own family, except under special conditions; before dinner he might indeed be said to be on the whole, rather curt than otherwise. Therefore, after divesting himself of his exterior garments, he now merely inquired in a casual way, as he strode along the lobby to go and dress for dinner, 'Is Tom come yet'? The answer was in the negative, but as Mrs. Crabbice well knew that her spouse was a punctual man at his dinner hour, as well as at all other times, she hurried away to see that the operations of the cook and tablemaid were in proper train. Her friendly chat with the Misses Crabbice, if not adjourned *sine die*, must not be resumed in Mr. Crabbice's august presence, at least, until fit occasion should present itself.

'Well, Tom,' said Mr. Crabbice to his highly esteemed son who had arrived just as dinner was going on, and was now busily engaged upon the wing of a fowl, while his sire having reached the last stage of his dessert, had got leisure and tone for a genial conversation. 'Well Tom, did you settle that matter of the Mill Inn?'

'Settle it! I say that Morris is a confounded sneak, and I always told you so.'

'Tom, when will you learn to speak in a rational way. Mind now, I've Edward Boyce's guarantee for him—or will have it, which is the same thing—and then the inventories. Mr. Boyce 'll be responsible for the whole value.'

'Stop, stop, governor, you're going a little too fast.'

'Why, you know Tom, though the fixed stock has decreased in value largely since that vagabond Adams went to the dogs, I'm not to lose by him.'

'Nor Morris either, I should say.'

'Well, nor Morris either. We'll give over an inventory at full value, as the furnishings stood, to Adams, and Mr. Boyce, with whom we'll really be dealing, and not with this young man, is too much of a gentleman to object or begin to chaffer about reductions.'

'I daresay he'll be saved the trouble, dad, so far as Morris is concerned.'

'What! you don't mean to say that he offered to insult Mr. Boyce with any of those fanatical notions that Dr. Graham mentioned?'

'I should think I meant to say pretty nigh all that,—could it ever have entered you head that this poor helpless pauper should begin by saying that his mental qualifications, and his physical disqualifications alike unfitted him for keeping an inn, and on our interrupting him—that is Edward and myself—with the assurance that the place could be managed by his mother and sister, if he would merely oversee the business, that he should end by declaring almost insolently, ''besides I object on principle, to selling spirituous liquors in any form whatever''.'

'And he refuses, point blank, then to accept this generous offer,' asked Mr. Crabbice, in the severest tone he could assume.

'Refuses! Aye, though you should offer to make him not only tenant but proprietor, in his own right, of the best hotel in Strathaven.'

Mr. Crabbice, Senior, was at the moment too replete in point of physical comfort to give way to extremely violent emotion; yet he lay back in his chair and gave two short and emphatic grunts —'Aye, aye. And it's no wonder if we're burdened with paupers and poor-rates. To think of a poor cripple, not worth a single penny in the world, refusing to be put in the way of gaining a respectable livelihood, for the sake of what he calls ''principle!'' —I call it moral cowardice.' And at this sounding phrase, Mr. Crabbice's face assumed an air of stern judicial gravity, while Mrs. Crabbice, lost in admiration of her husband's wisdom, and delighted at the coincidence of his opinion of Robert Morris with that she had herself so recently expressed, nodded to Miss Crabbice with a knowing and complacent smile, as much as to say, 'Didn't I tell you?'

'That's his temperance principles,' continued Mr. Crabbice—

'reject the undeserved kindness of people who would befriend him in a way he had no right to expect; and saddle the parish with a family of paupers. Talk of elevating the lower classes! The more one does for them the more ungrateful they become. I should like to know what Dr. Graham and Mr. Boyce will have to say for the manly and independent spirit of their *prottygee* now. However, it's as well we're rid of him. He has no further claim on my generosity now at least.'

'Advertise the Mill Inn to-morrow in the *Strathaven Independent*, dad,' said Mr. Crabbice's spirited son.

'Well said, Tom; and they shall soon see that it was no want of tenants that led me, at Mr. Boyce's urgent request, to make this liberal, but unbusinesslike offer.'

And so the advertisement was draughted, commencing in the usual form,

> TO LET, that eligible and well-frequented Hotel,
> so long known as the MILL INN, &c. &c.

As the *Independent* was published on the morrow, Tom Crabbice prepared to set off for Strathaven, with the injunction to see the advertisement put into the 'able editor's' own hands, after it had been revised by Lillie, the legal gentleman before mentioned, who might justly be described as 'a solicitor of all work', who now lived in a dingy room up two stairs, and whom Mr. Crabbice expected, from his known skill in these matters to 'put' the attractions of the Mill Inn as strongly as possible before the minds of prospective tenants without binding the proprietor to too much, in a legal sense.

'Don't be waiting me now, mamma,' said Tom Crabbice, as he put on his hat to leave for Strathaven, 'I've several calls to make and won't be home till it's late.'

Mrs. Crabbice expected as much from her former experience of Tom's habits; and she would have added some judicious advice on the subject, but Tom cut the legs from her opportunity by the promptitude of his departure, after he had uttered the sentences just given.

Chapter VII

A RETROSPECT—FILLING IN THE BACKGROUND

About the period in our history at which we have now arrived, the youthful laird of Drammochdyle had become a pretty frequent visitor at the manse of Strathaven, the situation and surroundings of which have been already described in a general way.

One ostensible cause of Edward Boyce's visits at the manse was to enjoy the society of Dr. Graham. And though the reader may believe that he knows of another cause, yet this was one which might have been urged with plausibility and with credit. For the parish minister of Strathaven *was* both 'a gentleman and a scholar'. Born of parents in the humblest ranks of life, he had, like many another Scottish youth, nobly fought his way onward; prosecuting a distinguished University career in the teeth of grinding poverty; the small pittances gained by private teaching in his spare hours serving to pay his class fees, to provide books, to pay the rent of a dismal little attic room, and to procure some oatmeal and a little milk—with scarcely anything besides—to maintain physical existence. Under this ordeal he had not only developed into a robust and handsome man physically, but cultivated his naturally excellent talents in no ordinary degree. Besides the learning that more especially belongs to his profession, he was master of more than one of the continental languages, had fine and cultured taste, both in poetry and music, and was no mean versifier.

Such was he when he undertook the 'cure of souls' at Strathaven; and, with an amiable and affectionate wife to share his lot, nothing seemed wanting to either his happiness or his usefulness. And for several years after his settlement, the minister of Strathaven was widely known as an eloquent preacher, while his constant and unwearied visitation of the sick and the poor among his people, and his generous interest in their welfare made him respected and beloved by all classes.

He was a man of eminently social character, keenly alive to the enjoyments of friendly intercourse; and hence it was that the manse of Strathaven was the frequent resort of many ever welcome visitors. And when his friends 'forgathered' at the manse, either at a formal 'party', or in a more free and easy style, whether they might chance to be wealthy farmers, shrewd business men, or those more specially of the educated classes, the minister had the power of making himself an agreeable companion to each and all—the purely unsophisticated of rustic training, as well as the cultured who knew 'the world', and its requirements and observances. Nor would he put them off with the mere charms of his conversation. They were freely invited to enjoy the pleasures of the social board. Sherry, port, and claret were set out for those who more affected gentility, and whisky toddy was ever at the command of the sturdy farmer or hardheaded tradesman when he called, and had time to combine business with pleasure. For himself, he might truly say that these beverages, one and all, were to him objects of indifference, or almost dislike. With the *mens sana in corpore sano* he felt neither the need of, nor the desire for, them. But who shall venture to say that he will make himself familiar with all or any of them, and yet keep them outside the circle of his habitual desires; or who, as a rational man, will even assert with confidence his ability to set a limit to that desire when once called into existence? By the time that the minister of Strathaven had received the degree of doctor in divinity, a degree justly earned by extensive and thorough scholarship, it was well enough known that, in respect to strong drink he was by no means an abstemious man. On the death of his wife shortly after, his grief found solace, as grief is wont to do in such circumstances, in deeper potations.

Had Dr. Graham been *now* what he was *once*, the fact of his being left sole guardian of an only and darling child, who was of an age to interest him by her companionship, and to engage his attention in her training, it would but have deepened his sense of responsibility, and made more earnest his resolution to keep before his mind and discharge aright the obligations resting upon him. And if a solemn shade had passed over him the effort to realise and adequately perform a sacred duty, would have brought its own rich reward. Of this, Dr. Graham was neither ignorant nor oblivious. Nor would it be true to say that he either wilfully neglected, or was indifferent to the well-being of his daughter Elsie. He was, indeed, doatingly fond of her, but his kindness was impulsive and fitful, rather than constant and unvarying in its action. A tyrant that would exact his own share of homage, had got possession of him; and the very sensitiveness and refinement of his mind but made him to feel the more keenly that there were seasons when it was not fit his guileless child should see too closely certain ruling features of her own father's life. It had come to this, that day by day, and every day, he felt his craving for the stimulus of strong drink too powerful to be resisted; and in seasons of excitement, of either a joyous or saddening character especially, he was helplessly carried on to that extent of indulgence which he himself felt to be, and his firmest friends at the social board failed not to mark and characterise on fit occasion, and with solemn shaking of the head, as— excess.

At such times as these, Dr. Graham could have wished Elsie— his own darling, Elsie—far from his presence. Nay, in the bitterness of his heart, he had actually sent her away to live at a distance, and be trained in household arts by a female relative of his own, though he felt the pang of parting even for a time most keenly, and moreover, he felt assured that the means for such training, and for her education generally, were less efficient than those presented at the Manse of Strathaven; had other things there been as they ought to have been. He had formed a vague resolution to curb the desire for strong drink, and to that end, proposed to commence at this time a couse of self-denying seclusion. The advice of his medical man was to break off gradually, from whisky toddy—or indeed, raw whisky—to which he had now advanced, by restricting himself to 'superior', wines, in whose 'generous' and 'nourishing' qualities the son of Esculapius had supreme faith. His science was not so profound as to have led him to a clear apprehension of the commonplace yet invariable and palpable fact that this 'generosity' consists simply in stealing away the man's senses with rather less violence; while their 'nourishing' powers point him in precisely the opposite direction from a diminution of either the quantity or force of his potations. That is supposing the patient to have even honestly carried the prescribed regime into practice, a thing that Dr. Graham certainly never succeeded in doing, if ever any man did.

Progress in intoxicating liquor in truth is not toward a diminishing and limited quantity; but toward a greater and unknown quantity. And so the minister of Strathaven found; for after a feeble effort at restraint, he gave way to indulgence more freely than before. Not that he ever, even yet, appeared in public in a state of intoxication. No; his excesses were more discreetly conducted than that.

And here is the main line of distinction between your toper in the better ranks of life and your toper in a humbler walk. The latter, from the very necessity of his position, swills and swills, wherever, whenever, and whatever he can get to drink, pouring raw whisky, of the most excoriating pungency, into an empty, or all but empty stomach; and he is next seen staggering through the streets; or he tumbles into the ditch, testifying to all men as openly as he can, what he is. But your respectable toper eschews, or professes to eschew, set drinking in the early part of the day; it is not 'the thing' to indulge then, except, it may be, to the extent of a quiet glass or two, swallowed *sub rosa*. But after a good dinner, he is your man for a stiff set to any day. And so Dr. Graham would sit for a couple of hours post-prandially mixing whisky and water, which he swallowed daily in greater quantity than would have sufficed to lay that poor, ragged, blear-eyed, drunken wretch in the gutter. Yet who should venture to say, in plain terms, that they ever saw him drunk?

Chapter VIII

THE RETROSPECT COMPLETED

In the circumstances already detailed, it had been with a feeling of something like relief that Dr. Graham, after Elsie's return home, had received into his family the orphan daughter of an old college companion. Agnes Wilson was Elsie's senior by about a twelvemonth. They were to pursue their education together, until Agnes might find some humble place as a teacher. Meanwhile, Strathaven Manse would be her home; and Dr. Graham felt that, in the warm-hearted, impulsive, yet thoughtful, Agnes, with her fair, open, cheerful face, his daughter had a pure and guileless companion in those hours when he would rather be alone.

The years passed on, and when the accident occurred that deprived Robert Morris of a limb, the girls at the manse were of the ages of seventeen and eighteen respectively. That sad story had reached Strathaven manse in due course. Indeed, it was carried thither at first by Agnes and Elsie, who had heard it when out visiting among the poor. Dr. Graham, on hearing of the accident and its consequences, expressed his pity, and, as he scarcely knew Robert as a parishioner, let it slip from his mind again.

Sometime after, the two young ladies recalled his attention to the unfortunate affair, and somewhat indirectly proposed that he should visit Robert.

'Morris—that's the family who live in the feus by the edge of the common?' said Dr. Graham.

'Yes, uncle,' was Agnes's reply, 'and you must recollect poor Robert who worked at the repairs on the manse last summer.'

'Oh, the lad that one day maintained stiff argument with me upon the principle of a State-paid Church, and so forth. Dissenter—and consequently half-heretic—as he was, he seemed to find favour with Elsie and you, Aggie!'

'And I'm sure he would with you, if you once knew him rightly,' said Elsie.

'How do you come to that conclusion, Elsie?'

'Because he's much more intelligent than the young men of the parish, generally. He reads a great deal, and thinks for himself.'

'Ah! but that's dangerous, isn't it, when young men—or young women either—read the wrong books, perhaps, and then begin to think on the material thus gathered?'

'Well,' said Agnes slyly, 'He just needs you at this very time to keep him right. He has read all his own books, and all ours, too, long ago; and so let my wise uncle step in with his safe books and sage counsels!'

'You little hussy,' said Dr. Graham—who at the moment was himself in one of his best moods—patting Agnes on the cheek, 'you would have me not only allow you to visit outlandish persons who decline to join themselves to my flock, but to stoop from my official dignity, and do so myself. Well, as you wish it, I suppose I must.'

'Not "must"; but of course you will!'

'Weel, weel, lassie, ye're a sma' tyrant in your way,' was the reply.

And Dr. Graham did so; and visited oftener than once. He found the young man, on better acquaintance, neither fanatical nor arrogantly talkative on religious subjects, as he had pictured him, in accordance with the popular notion of the conventional dissenter, but modest and intelligent on general subjects. His interest in Robert Morris increased; he lent him books from his library, and when Robert was so far recovered as to be able to limp about on crutches, he made him call daily at the manse to receive lessons from himself in grammar and other subjects. And concurrently with his own visits, he sent Elsie or her companion to minister in various kind offices to the family, as occasion served.

On one of her earlier visits at widow Morris's cottage. Elsie Graham accidentally met Edward Boyce, and the sequel was what Eliza Crabbice had pictured, with perhaps no greater additions than were to be expected by the time the tale had passed through two or three hands; such as those of Mrs. Ellison, or the Howdie, or Johnnie Duncan, receiving a slight touch in the way of embellishment from each. Yet, it was not an unnatural thing that Edward Boyce on being thus thrown into the companionship of Elsie Graham, should willingly avail himself of the opportunity to renew an acquaintance which had been broken off for several years, by his attendance at college, and her absence from her father's dwelling; nor was it, perhaps, very unnatural that the friendship should become a somewhat intimate and cordial one; for Elsie Graham was now a blooming, nay, even handsome, and womanly-looking girl, and it were too much to suppose that Edward Boyce was so engrossed with aught else as to be impervious to female charms.

And, though anticipating history a little, let it be said that matters had, in fact, gone faster and farther than even the watchful Mrs. Crabbice dreamt of; and her little scheme on behalf of her dear Eliza, was almost hopeless, by the time she had set about making a formal attempt to bring it into effective operation.

When the party met at Vatville, as already spoken of, it was hardly a matter of doubt with Edward Boyce that Elsie Graham should be his wife. His plans for the future were, perhaps, not quite clearly defined, but the thing resolved itself mainly into a question, of when the house of Drammochdyle should be completely finished, so as the marriage of its owner might be gone about with due pomp, and a fitting house be ready for his bride.

Chapter IX

EDUCATIONAL

The average Scotch parish Dominie, of twenty to twenty-five years ago, was a sad abortion professionally considered. At least, such was the opinion Robert Morris formed of the class, from the fact that, as a little boy, he had attended two of them in succession—men who stood rather high in public estimation as teachers too—and left both at the age of fourteen with such school education as he was likely ever to get, completed, without having learnt one single thing thoroughly or intelligently. To be sure he liked fun, trifling, and mischief, as much as most boys, but he was not naturally a dunce, and the absurdity of it was that while he maintained, without courting it, the reputation of being one of the best scholars (such *bestness* as there can be among a parcel of disorderly laddies of thirteen or fourteen), he was all the while bilking the dominie to a most enormous extent, and slimming his tasks in a style that was positively disgraceful. Repeating the grammar lesson day by day, yet hardly ever once looking into the pages of Lennie, a judicious practice, assiduously pursued, of laying his lugs in his neck while the two or three 'Latiners', whom he prudently kept between him and the 'head' of the grammar class, were parrot-like conjugating the verb, which he knew he would have to do next in exactly the same style, serving for the acquisition of the morning's task. And in like manner had the Maister asked him to decline *'penna* a pen', or conjugate *amo*, he could have done it to about equally good purpose, for when tired of guessing the way to 'state' some question in proportion, which he was sure to light upon at last by close scrutiny of the 'Answer'

37

duly set down in 'the Gray' before him, it was on the whole rather
interesting as a change to listen to the privileged loons, who were
to be the dominies and parsons of the future, labouring away '*hic-
hæec-hoc*', and, as he deemed it, very like their work at the pages
of Ruddiman. Truly it *was* shameful waste of time all this, with
the addition of reading chap books furtively, and drawing gro-
tesque and not creditable sketches on his slate; but we presume
it is in boy nature, even yet, to follow similar courses if allowed,
and what veneration is due to the memory of those constituent
members of 'our admirable parochial system', under whom it
was possible; or what part of the responsibility attached to teacher
and taught respectively, we need not inquire.

But when Robert Morris, under Dr. Graham's rational
instruction, and his own independent and earnest application,
began really to get firm hold of principles, he then saw clearly
enough what a botched and abortive business his early schooling
had been, and could appreciate the huge advantage they possess
whose time, up to early manhood, has been occupied by sys-
tematic and thorough training.

His formal education, to speak with anything like correctness,
had only begun in those months when he was recovering his
health and strength. And concurrently with the regular instructions of his Rev. preceptor, other educational agencies were at
work. There were the visits of the two young ladies from the
manse. Cultivated and intelligent as they were, their influence
could not, and did not, go for nothing, on a nature open and
unsuspecting, and ready at least to appreciate real refinement,
apart from a pretentious gentility, essentially false, or a shallow
sentimentality as selfish as specious.

And about this time a close companion of Robert's was James
Monro, a working engineer, who had recently come to fulfil an
engagement at the small Strathaven foundry. He was rather
Robert's junior in years, but had seen a little more of the world
than he, and his ardent impulsive temperament made him ever
ready not only to express his opinion or discuss a point, but it
might be occasionally to dogmatise rather stoutly; while his
undoubted clearness of head, and force of intellect, gave him a
wholesome, incisive, and stimulating power over his friend.

Chapter X

STRATHAVEN MANSE—
AN INTERIOR SCENE

Robert Morris had continued to call almost daily upon Dr. Graham. He was an assiduous, if not brilliant student, and his unflagging industry accomplished tasks that made his preceptor look with satisfaction on his progress, a satisfaction to which he was not slow to give expression.

On two or three occasions, Robert Morris, who always called at the Manse in the early part of the day, had been told that Dr. Graham was ill, and that he could not see him. At first he had ventured in the succeeding interview to ask particularly after the Dr.'s health, but this was taken with so evident an air of something like irritability, that he thereafter forbore the slightest allusion to the subject. On calling a few days after the party at Mr. Crabbice's, at which he and his affairs had been discussed, and which had led to his being nominated tenant-prospective of the Mill Inn, Robert received from Elsie, whose face was flushed as if she had been recently crying, the former statement that her father was not well, and could not be seen. Robert rose directly to leave, wondering what *might* be troubling Elsie, who was so dispirited and restrained in her manner; and Agnes Wilson had broken in with a remark or two designed to turn the conversation to a former subject of discussion amongst the three, and relieve the embarrassment of her companions, when Dr. Graham's bell was rung vehemently. Elsie hurried off to answer the summons, and directly thereafter Robert Morris heard something like words of altercation between Dr. Graham and his daughter, and amidst which his own name was repeated with the exclamation from the Dr. in excited tones—'But I *will* see him. I know he's here; send him to me now.'

Poor Robert stood in a half-bewildered state. He could have wished himself anywhere save in the Manse of Strathaven; but of what use? He was utterly confounded, and as a last resort cast an earnest imploring look in Agnes Wilson's quietly expressive face. Her straighforward, though sadly silent look in return, accompanied by a slight but perceptible shake of the head, somehow—in a way that he did not expect, and could not explain—went far to restore Robert to entire calmness, and manly self-possession.

Presently Elsie returned, 'My father insists on seeing you Robert,' exclaimed the poor girl, almost sobbing, 'and he's not right. Edward Boyce and Tom Crabbice were here last night at dinner; and staid too late, and poor father—Oh, Robert, I know you will never speak of it. These late hours are too much for him now, and he has been taking wine already. But go, Robert, he is in his study, and will be out after me if we keep him waiting.'

With no little reluctance, Robert made the best of his way to the study, where he found Dr. Graham pacing the floor with his face unusually flushed.

'Come away Mr. Morris—sit down now, I want to speak to you,' said Dr. Graham, in a hurried, half angry, half jocular tone. 'What's this you've been about man—quarrelling with your sole means of making a livelihood, Eh?'

'Is it Mr. Crabbice's Inn you're speakin' o' Sir?' asked Robert.

'Crabbice's Inn? Aye; to be sure. The Mill Inn. Would it not have been a good thing for your Mother's family, to have been comfortably set down there?'

'I think not, Sir.'

'You think not. Eh? But are you the best judge, young man?'

'I can judge of what's right'——

'Ah, ah, you'll be telling me about your principles and all that; and that it's right in the teeth of these. I don't want to hear about that. You should consider what a young man in your circumstances is to do.'

'Well, I have considered, and I'll not do *that* though I should carry a pedlar's box. And besides, it would be a bad speculation to any one who had no scruples of conscience.'

'Bad; why bad?'

'Because the terms offered by Mr. Crabbice are not fair'——

'Take care, young man,' exclaimed Dr. Graham, emphatically, 'That's too much; for a friendless youth to speak that way of a man of Mr. Crabbice's position and influence. He was willing to befriend you, Sir, and you've offended him. And you've offended Mr. Boyce, too, by the rude and unpolite way in which you replied to Mr. Tom, when he made this offer—was that right, sir?'

'Dr. Graham,' said Robert Morris, with the emphasis of unwonted excitement, 'I have my ain convictions o' duty in this matter; and I say that though I should gain my bread by selling brooms through the country, I'll never consent to gain't by selling that which degrades alike the vendor and the purchaser. But I must deny that I spoke with rudeness or incivility to Mr. Crabbice's son. So far fae that, I tried at least, however akwardly, to .express my gratitude, especially to Mr. Boyce, for his generosity, though I could not avail mysel' o't.'

'D'ye mean to question my words in my own house, Sir? D'ye mean—I say, d'ye mean to make imputations on me?' exclaimed Dr. Graham, getting very purple in the face, and drawing himself up before Robert.

'I beg your pardon, Sir. Far be it from me to cast imputations on you, who have been my best friend. I owe you a debt of gratitude I can never'—

'Now, just stop that,' said Dr. Graham, changing his tone all at once. 'But, Robert, you are unreasonable. I—I fear I cannot be of any further service to you. You've offended Crabbice—I can't afford to offend Crabbice. And you've offended Edward Boyce. And Tom Crabbice—ah, he has us all by the ears. I was just afraid of it, and warned them. But, no no; I didn't expect such a bad blow up as this.'

'I hope, Sir, you'll think nane the worse o' me for acting conscientiously.'

'None; not I, young man. But you need friends; and you have acted imprudently—very imprudently.'

'I am sorry you should think so; but I couldna do otherwise.'

'Well, well, I believe you. Still, it was cutting off the sinews of war. I could once face poverty without fear, and lie under obligation to none; perhaps you are right. Go home, Robert, and

God bless you,' added Dr. Graham, as he shook hands with Robert, and bade good bye in a tone still excited, but very different from that in which he opened the colloquy.

Chapter XI

FACING THE WORLD—
A NEW START IN LIFE

The thoughts and feelings of Robert Morris as he pursued his way homeward to his mother's cottage, after his interview with Dr. Graham, were by no means of the brightest or most hopeful cast. Long ere this, the question of how he was to gain a living for himself, and provide for his mother had been the subject of anxious thought. And the lessons he had been receiving from Dr. Graham, had been eagerly pursued not alone for their own sake, but as furnishing him with a power whereby he might do some useful work of a different, and mayhap of a higher kind than had ever before engaged his energies. It had been his ambition to qualify himself as a teacher; but after what had just taken place, the conviction seized upon him that with a kindness, for which he felt truly grateful, both Dr. Graham and Edward Boyce looked upon him as so far a burden which it was desirable to be rid of as soon as might be.

He resolved to start forthwith in search of employment, and also to accept whatever might turn up, provided it implied nothing dishonourable, and offered the prospect of the barest subsistence; for the idea of remaining for even a short time longer in a position to invite the benevolence of those who had befriended him appeared now to be intolerable.

The only friend he had now to consult was James Munro, and James's counsels were called in accordingly.

'Gae an' offer yersel' as manager o' the new Strathaven Gas Work,' said James. 'The place is advertised vacant in the *Independent*!'

'The joke's rather owre grim, Jamie, for a man that sees actually naething atween 'im an' the status o' legal pauper.'

'But its nae joke—it's sober earnest, Bob.'

'An' dee ye actually mean to say that I sud gang an' pit *my* name to the list o' half a score that we ken to be already seekin' the place?'

'An' why not?'

'Weel I dinna need ance erran' to make mysel' ridiculous.'

'Listen to me, noo Bob.—Tell me if you can, hoo mony o' the half score candidates are better qualified than yoursel?'

'Weel some o' them are nane better—that's true aneuch.'

'Nane o' them are better. I ken something o' the entire lot—ye only want sufficient impudence to push yer claims, man.'

'I fear there's another element o' success wantin', an' which canna be so readily picke't up—influence.'

'Deed I daursay ye're no far oot there. That's the curse o' yer bits o' sma' toonies especially. There's never an openin' occurs worth ha'ein', but there's some drucken, blethrin', half broken doon "local man" needin' the job; wi freen's ready to stap him in neck an' heels; or some brainless young goose whose fader happens to be brither to a bailie, or siclike—he'll gae in, ass that he be, against the best qualified man in the universe.'

'So you think my chance wud be very encouragin' I daursay!'

'Weel, I suppose I've raither upset my ain argument, Bob. But lat me assure you that a good stock of cool impudence, an' some tact—for a man needs to be discreetly impudent—gae far in carryin' a man through the warld. I'm nae an aul' man yet, but I've seen *that* mair that ance successfu' against fat seem'd great odds.'

'Aye, but then it's been impudence against merit only—nae impudence against local 'influence'; but fat gars ye denounce sma' toonies in particular—doesna influence operate in the same way in the case of big toons?'

'Scarcely; ye see in the like of Strathaven they're a' linkit thegither in bits o' cliques an' family relationships. An' fan an openin' occurs, an' some gawpus that happens to hae a fader or an uncle o' some standin', casts his ee upon't; or his mither thinks 'This wud dee richt weel wi' oor Johnny'—or his daddy is feelin' tiret o' mainteenin' the useless howffin—forthwith the strings begin to be pull't. This man can get the Baillie's lug, an' that the Shirra's—I can sair your business a gweed turn, an' maybe ye cud dee mine a bad ane; so that the hail local circle is secured; or at least a "workin' majority". Noo in big toons it's impossible to get the en's o' a' the strings in your ain han'. An' so merit may hae some chance. In sma' toons it has nane.'

'Severe aneuch surely, Jamie. But I fear we're gettin' raither general. So, b'yer leave, I think I maun direct a little attention to my ain particular case. Folk get selfish, ye ken, fan their ain sma' concerns press.'

'Twere needless to tell of Robert's experiences in search of a situation. How many people were applied to and declined his services, some with a gratuitous bluntness and incivility, that inflicted on the applicant an amount of needless pain and humiliation that might have made even the authors of it sorry had they been aware of its extent; others with apologetic expressions of regret, that so far at least softened the refusal; while one or two tender hearted people promised to 'keep him in mind', when they should 'hear of anything'; a tolerably safe, but in the general run of events, singularly unfruitful sort of promise.

And Robert's appreciation of the truth of the saying that 'hope deferred maketh the heart sick', had begun to get more vivid than pleasant, when, through the medium of his old master, Mr. Barkus, he was introduced to Mr. Patten, managing partner of the firm of Patten, Pendicle, & Co., timber merchants, and shipping agents, &c., who were in want of a clerk. Mr. Patten was one of the leading philanthropists in Strathaven; and, indeed, gave away a goodly sum of money yearly for benevolent purposes. He was one of a class of philanthropists not quite unknown in other regions besides that of Strathaven. That is to say, his charity flowed mainly in certain recognised and orthodox channels, and within the banks of these, it not unfrequently assumed the form of a stream, large enough to fructify and refresh; but attempt to turn it into another course that had not directly religious—perhaps rather demonationally religious, or other orthodox authentication—and unless strong pressure were used, it was apt to fall away, until it bore quite as much resemblance to the unblessed water spilt upon the ground. He was a Dissenter, and, of course, a leading member of the 'Church' at Strathaven; and as such, knew something of Robert Morris, whom he received very blandly—(as, indeed, Mr. Patten received everybody)—as he looked up from the desk in his queer, cramped, little office, which in its normal condition afforded room for only about three people to sit or stand in it; the remainder of the space being occupied with lumber of every conceivable kind, including various specimens of sawn timber from the Baltic, and North American forests.

'And Mr Barkus told you we were requiring a clerk?' observed Mr. Patten in a semi-interrogatory sort of way.

'Yes, sir,' answered Robert. 'He asked me to call upon you and enquire about it.'

'Yes—very worthy man Mr. Barkus. You were in his employ formerly?'

'Yes.'

'Well, you see my partner Mr. Pendicle is getting frail, and is able to be but little in the office—old age creeps upon us all you know—and we wish a young man who has a good hand at the pen, and is expert at figures, to keep the books, look after unloading cargoes sometimes, and attend public sales, and so on. Have you a good knowledge of book-keeping?'

'I understan' the principles well enough to keep ordinary books, I think. I have had no practice.'

'Ah—no of course; but practice would be got with a little time. You write a good hand—yes, to be sure, Mr. Barkus showed me your letter to him. And you would be willing to make yourself generally useful in the business?'

'I can honestly promise that, sir; an' I'll do my best to learn everything that I may be deficient in.'

'Well, I'll consult Mr. Pendicle—yes, but about the salary. We had thought of just apprenticing a bit boy, for really the times are hard, and there's so many claims of a pressing kind now. I, just not an hour ago, set down our name for an annual sub-scription of two guineas, for the Feejee Mission. Ye see, we could hardly think of giving more than five shillings a-week to begin with.'

'Well, sir,' answered Robert with at least outward composure. 'I will leave that part entirely to yourselves, I'll be but too glad to get an openin' where I can honestly earn something, however sma'.'

'Very well, very well. I'll consult Mr. Pendicle, and let you hear to-morrow—Good day.'

And he did so, the result being that the worthy firm agreed to offer Robert a year's engagement, the terms being on the one part, a payment of six shillings weekly—the firm advanced a shilling you see—and on the other, twelve hours labour daily in the interest of Messrs. Patten & Pendicle.

The offer was at once accepted, and Robert Morris thereafter became the recognised occupant of the well-worn desk at which Mr. Pendicle had operated, more or less, for the bye-gone forty years.

Chapter XII

NEW PROSPECTS FOR TWO CONTEMPORARIES

It did not need a very great event to form a topic of general conversation in the Kirktoon of Strathaven, and we presume the remark applies to Kirktowns in general. Anyhow, Robert Morris had barely arranged to enter upon a new line of duties, when he awoke to find himself famous. Johnny Duncan, in the course of his travels, had 'gotten't i' the the toon' that very night, and of course the intelligence was speedily in circulation.

'I tell't ye the lad wud come to something yet,' added Johnny.

'To be a clerk!' exclaimed Mrs. Muggart, 'na sirs, but's mither will be thinkin' 'ersel' up-by-cairts noo.'

'He has a good heed; there's no fear o' 'im,' pursued the beadle.

'I aye thocht 'im owre fond o' lear for the squar-wrichtin.'

'Fats that noo!' exclaimed Mrs. Slorach, the smith's wife, who popped her head—followed by her portly person—into Mrs. Muggart's ben end, at the moment.

'Come awa, Mrs. Slorach, I wus jist tellin' 'er 't Robbie Morris 's gotten a gran' sittivation.'

'Na, maister Duncan, but that *is* news,' replied Mrs. Slorach.

The howdie looked glum at Johnny's too prompt announcement, as she would rather willingly have been the first bearer of the tidings to Mrs. Slorach herself. However, the secret was out now, and she must do the best she could. So she broke in—

'Noo, Mrs. Slorach, wusna we jist speakin' the ither nicht hoo weel mithna some o' the muckle fowk gie Robbie a bearth, an' sae cawpable 's he wud be for't?'

'Ay, deed wus we oman, for I aye thocht Robbie an uncommon clever lad, fatever some fowk did.'

The truth was, the two worthy souls were now as eager to join in Johnny's vaticinations as to Robert's brilliant future, as they had been formerly to join in that worthy's series of prophecies about him, as the 'poor gone lad', who was speedily to find a lair in the quiet churchyard. And no doubt they were just as sincere in the one case as the other.

Next day they encountered each other in Mrs. Morris's, whither—moved by kindred impulses—they had happened to go at the same time, to congratulate her on her son's good fortune; and there also was Mrs. Ellison, the souter's wife.

'Aye, Robbie lad!' exclaimed the howdie, 'we'll maybe see the day that ye'll be provost o' Strathaven yet, or a baillie at the verra least.'

'Ye expect to be a lang liver, than,' said Robert with the air of one not a little amused, and quietly effecting his retreat from the matronly conclave.

'Tut man,' pursued the worthy dame, as he rather unceremoniously disappeared, ostensibly to do some piece of not very important work, 'fa kens; "faint heart never wan fair lady", an' that min's me o' yer auld cronie, Geordie Ross; ye'll ken that he's to be marriet in a fortnicht come Saturday first.'

'Geordie Ross to be married in a fornicht!' echoed Mrs. Ellison, 'keep's 'oman, an' fa till?'

Mrs. Muggart knew that she had exclusive possession of a piece of stirring news this time, and she was not disposed to part with it too freely, like a reckless spendthrift; so she answered one question by putting another. 'Dear me, Mrs. Ellison, an' dinna ye ken that? I wager Mrs. Slorach kens.'

'Deed no, Eppie,' said that worthy dame bluntly, 'I get but fyou o' the kwintra clyps.'

'Na, Mrs. Muggart, but it's you that hears the news', said Mrs Ellison, 'as may weel beseem ye; "A gaun fit's aye gettin'"' as they say.'

'A gaun fit!' exclaimed the howdie, in well-feigned astonishment. 'An' some folk appears to ken but little o' fat their neist door neebours are deein'. 'Kwintra clyps!' It needs but sma' traivel to get *that* Mrs. Ellison. Gin folk could but keep their e'en open.'

'Sirs! fa cud it be noo?' said the souter's wife in an agony of suspense.

'I'se warrant ye Geordie thinks he's a lucky man,' pursued Mrs. Muggart, 'though there's *some* fowk no sae weel pleas't, I doot. Hooever, we can but ''dae as we dow''; and if fowk will fesh up their bairns to follow their ain gate, in fatever else they like, they canna expect them to dee itherweese i' their marryin'.'

'It canna be Kate Reid, the deacon's daachter,' queried Mrs. Ellison, driven almost to desperation.

'An' fat for no,' calmly replied the howdie. 'The deacon, nae doot, thocht to get a walthy man for a sin-in-law. ''Like draws to like'', ye see; but we canna aye get what we wud mak a bode for. So he maun eyven be content wi' Geordie Ross—a peer journeyman squarwright.'

'Na, but ye *dee* astonish me, Mrs. Muggart. O' a' the marriages I *hae* heard tell o'; but *hoo* they managed to keep it so quaet! I never liket that marriages 't braks oot wi' a suddenty that gate,' added the souter's wife gravely.

'A suddenty!' exclaimed Mrs. Muggart scornfully, and disposed now to draw the long bow a little. 'Bless *me*, 'oman, it's been o' the irons this sax month, to *my* kennin'. Forbye that, it's nearhan' a raith sin' that toitlin bodie, Johnny Duncan, wus claverin' 't ower the haill pairis.'

'Heely, heely noo Mrs. Muggart, for Johnny Duncan wus in wi' a pair o' Sunday spats that he's been makin' to my man this sax month—sicklike makin' as they've gotten—gweed claith spoil't jist—muckle better till's employt' a tailor that cud dee's wark the richt gate. He was in nae langer gane nor the nicht afore the streen, an fient a cheep was in's head aboot the marriage. Noo, if he hed a' kent, he cudna but a tell't's, for he sat near an hoor discoorsin wi' mysel' an' 'Peter thegither.'

The facts adduced were rather against the howdie. However, she evaded that point with her usual dexterity, and went on to the next. Only the continuation of the conversation need not be recorded. The circumstances were these—Deacon Reid, a rather elderly, and partially-retired tradesman of the cooper craft, had an only daughter, Kate; and the deacon being a reputedly very wealthy man, and Kate a good-looking young lass, she was greatly talked of among a certain section of the beaus in and about Strathaven. The howdie and souter's wife had correctly enough interpreted the deacon's views relative to the prospects of his daughter in the article of matrimony. He being a man worth about a thousand pounds probably—the fruits of hard work and close saving—imagined it to be a right and becoming thing that Kate as the family representative should be mated with one of corresponding monetary status. In other respects, there was no inequality that could well be alleged; for Kate was of no higher blood, and no greater refinement than her sweetheart. Yet when George Ross's successful courtship of Kate became suddenly known, her father, for the sole reason stated, got very angry; and remained very sulky indeed for a number of days. But it was of no use; as why should it be, Kate would not be swayed; and at last a rather sour parental consent was given to the marriage.

Chapter XIII

THE MILL INN AND ITS NEW TENANT

In the weekly number of the *Strathaven Independent*, of date April 16th, 18—, the community received this initimation:

MILL INN

GEORGE ROSS begs to inform the Nobility, Gentry, and Commercial Public and Community in general, that he has taken a Lease of that long established and favourite Hotel, known as the MILL INN.

G. R., in soliciting a continuance of that support so liberally bestowed upon his predecessor, begs to assure those who may favour him with their Patronage, that no exertion shall be wanting on his part to secure their approbation and increased countenance; for which purpose he has laid in a large Stock of the best Spirits, Wines, Liqueurs, &c., &c.

N.B.—Fine old Strathaven Whiskies, unparalleled for Toddy. Breakfasts, Dinners, &c., with smart waiters. Posting in all its departments, with fast horses and steady drivers.

So Mr. Crabbice, after a somewhat strenuous effort, had at last got a suitable tenant for the Mill Inn. And not many days after the foregoing announcement had been made to the world, the new tenant (though an old acquaintance of ours) might have been seen bustling about his 'premises', endeavouring to acquire that air of unproductive activity which 'mine host' loveth to wear. As he was thus usefully employed, Mr. Tom Crabbice turned the corner into the courtyard with a familiar. 'Well, Ross, how are you getting on—everything in tip-top order now, I suppose?'

'Oh, we're doin' pretty well, Sir; but it takes a dale o' thocht to get a' thing to richts,' replied the innkeeper, with that semi-deferential, unassured air, which some of those who, as workmen *amongst* workmen assume to be staunch democrats—not to say levellers—do put on when face to face with one who is a little above them in social life.

'I say, Ross,' continued Mr. Tom, after a little, 'you're a confoundedly lucky fellow to hook such a strapping wench as Kate Reid for your wife.' The polite remark was no doubt suggested by the appearance of the newly-made Mrs. Ross passing at the other side of the court-yard. Strange to say, George Ross, in place of resenting the impertinent familiarity, smiled an unmanly smile, and merely said, 'Aw dinna ken', as Tom Crabbice went on:—

'And, better still, with lots of tin—an only daughter too. By jingo, you'll get all the old cove has some day.'

'Weel, it needs nae little to furnish oot a place like this, Sir—I could'na believed'—

'Tut, but then it's only once to do. And once set a-going, you've only to keep the ball rolling, d'ye see. Now, I say, Ross,' added Tom, changing his strain somewhat abruptly, 'of course, I don't want you to deceive my governor—that's the old man, you know—but you and I will understand each other in a thing or two; and if I should happen to be here sometimes when he imagines that I am elsewhere—at home in my bed, for example—there's no use in him knowing anything of that kind. Eh?'

'You mean, when you call here, Sir?'

'Of course, I do; it might suit my fancy not to be quite so early to bed some evenings, as the old folks would think becoming and decorous. Important engagement might keep me out late, you know. Now, if I should call here sometimes with a friend or two a little after business hours—Mum—d'ye understand—with the governor? I'll do as much for you.'

The new hotel keeper, whose moral stamina was not of the most robust order, at once succumbed to this degrading proposition, as he 'mumbled' out a sort of affirmative.

'And mind you have a drop of good liquor on hand always to give us.'

'Oh, the whisky is a' fae the Strathaven distillery—I think it's first-rate.'

'No doubt; but, bless me. Ross, you don't mean to say that you'll give all your customers the genuine article! You *must* have it good for people who know a thing or two. But suit your goods to your customer, you observe. That's the ticket, if you wish to thrive. There's such a mixture as 'kill the carter', you know, cheaply concocted, yet with a powerful grip, to please your brazen-throated coal-heavers, and such like.'

'Aye, I ken there's better an' waur fusky, as weel as ither things.'

'I say, Ross', continued Mr. Tom Crabbice 'that's a splendid bay mare I bought for you. Dog cheap at the money. Are you going to invest in another to match her?'

'Na: I think no, Sir. Ye see we've but sma' chance o' postin' jobs here; an' the beast we've gotten for the spring-cart an' the heavy wark 'll tak the side o' the chaise at a pinch when it *is* needit. The warst is he has nae tail nor mane, an' the mare has a swingin' tail—to her verra heels. They'll no jist be verra weel match't.'

'I should think not. And the brute has a greased leg, and feet as broad and flat as a wooden trencher.'

'Weel they're nae jist sae snod as they micht be; but he's tyeuch for a' that—capital stuff.'

'An' what about your driver? I see you've kept on that old heavy drunken fellow, Davie Beaton, as hostler.'

'Weel, Sir, ye see Davie was uncommon weel kent amo' the customers at the Mill Inn, an' weel liket; an' I was advised that it would be a wise thing to keep him on.'

'A wise thing to keep *him* on?'

'Aye, aye, some o' the regular aul' stagers like aye to ca' in about Davie fan they come up, ye see.'

'Oh! to call Davie in to wet his thrapple when they're taking a caulker?'

'Aye; he's weel respeckit that way; an' syne he has sic a' foond o' droll stories and siclike.'

'Droll stories! Hang it, I never saw him sit ten minutes on end till he's dead asleep. He's surely the last man to tell stories.

"With a headpiece as hollow as an empty brass kettle,
And a visage well sheath'd in the same very mettle".'

'I mean he's kent a' the maist humoursome customers about the place for mony a lang, an' they like to keep up the splore wi' Davie.'

'Well—but have you no other man-servant. You should go ahead and get a smart fellow to drive.'

'Raelly the place cudna afford it,' answered George, with more decision than he had hitherto shown in his discourse with Mr. Tom.

'Well, well, Ross. You know best yourself. But mind yon part of it.'

And Tom Crabbice was off for the time, leaving the new tenant of the Mill Inn to mind his own affairs.

Chapter XIV

THE LAIRD OF DRAMMOCHDYLE'S MARRIAGE—THE REJOICINGS

In a symmetrically constructed story, it would be absolutely outrageous to consign two of the principal characters to the commonplace region of married life with scarcely the slightest attempt at illustrating either the philosophy or the romance of love and courtship. That part of the performance will, however, come in due course. Meantime, as events in actual life do not fall out in the order of an 'artistically' devised story, we shall stick to the dry facts of history. And here our attention is arrested by a prominent paragraph in the pages of an elderly number of a journal to which we are mightily indebted in the compilation of these sketches. It runs thus—

'We understand that about the end of the ensuing month of July, Edward Boyce, Esq. of Drammochdyle, who has just returned from an absence of several months in the metropolis arranging family affairs, will lead to the hymeneal altar Miss Elspet E. F. G. Graham, the only, lovely, and accomplished daughter of the Rev. John G. Graham, A.M., D.D., parochial clergyman of Strathaven.'

A month later the same organ spoke in this wise—

'The arduous and indefatigable labours of the spirited and energetic committee, under the able convenership of Mr. Castock, farmer, Barreldykes, promise to render this enthusiastic and spontaneous demonstration in honour of the nuptials of the public-spirited proprietor of Drammochdyle and his lovely and accomplished bride, one of the most gratifying ovations ever rendered to a country gentleman.' So said the *Independent*, in its anticipatory article, headed the

'APPROACHING GREAT MARRIAGE RE-JOICINGS.'

We do not know whether George Ross, the new landlord of the Mill Inn might not have been in a position slightly to modify this rather glowing description. For, as the committee meetings were held in the landlord's private room of his hostelry, and as he was called in for consultation and advice upon practical points, he knew, as matter of fact, that the 'able convener, Mr. Castock', who was chairman prospective, as being principal tenant upon the estate of Drammochdyle, and the able vice-convener, Mr. Pattle of Gouckstyle, who was the croupier prospective, had quarrelled and come to high words about the cost and conditions of the dinner. Mr. Castock urged that the 'genteel' style of going through with it was to charge the dinner tickets at half-a-guinea each, and say 'wines included', while Mr. Pattle declared emphatically that at that cost one-half of the tenantry would have nothing to do with the dinner.

'Na, na,' said he, 'nane o' yer high flown affairs, Barreldykes; five shillins is aneuch, in a' conscience, to pay for denner an' a dram. An' lat ilka man get drink for himsel', accordin' till's nain drooth. Forbye 't there 'll be the fiddlers and a batch o' ither trumpery to pay for. I'se warran' the comma-tee 'll ken o't ere a' be deen.'

'It says little for the public spirit o' the tenans o' a man like Mr. Boyce to hear ony o' them speak that gate, Mr. Pattle,' observed the able convener, with a disdainful sneer.

Mr. Pattle was a man of keen temper, and he retorted, with considerable warmth, that Drammochdyle and all his belongings micht gae to Birse for him, ere he wud herry 'imsel for them.

'I'll be shot if I pay mair nor five shillins,' said he. 'The haill thing is a skaim o' yer nain, Barrels, to haud in wi' the gentry, an' force yersel' forrat as cheerman.'

'Wheesht, wheesht, men,' interposed a judicious committee-man, who observed that the convener's countenance was assuming a very explosive aspect, 'it'll never dee to quarrel noo, fan the thing's gane sae far. For my ain pairt, I saw little eese o' ever proposin' sic an expense for a't we're behadden to oor lairds, Jist lat the tickets be a croon the piece. Gin ye mak them the dooble, an' affoord drink, I'll be boon' the innkeeper 'll hae less profit nor gin ye tak five shillins and gar ilka ane pay for his nain tipple —an' that's no sayin' that some o' *them* will save siller either.'

With a sullen assent from the 'able convener', this compromise was accepted and the details settled.

George Ross and his wife, amid much sweat and perplexity, did their best to provide for the vigorous appetites of five dozen of farmers and country tradesmen; and they had their reward, inasmuch as it was duly put on record that 'mine host and hostess of the Mill Inn did their part to admiration, supplying a dinner of the most sumptuous character. The viands were superb, and admirably served, while the *liqueurs* were of the most *recherché* description'.

Of the dinner proceedings generally, we need only to give a very brief summary, from the able and impartial local journal which duly informed the public of Strathaven that 'the duties of the chair were most efficiently discharged by Mr. Castock, supported, right and left, by Rev. Dr. Graham, Messrs. Crabbice, sen. and jun., Captain Ryrie, and other neighbours and friends of the family; while Mr. Pattle made an excellent croupier'. 'The usual loyal and patriotic toasts' having been 'duly honoured', the Chairman requested the company to fill 'a very special bumper'. 'Gentlemen,' said Mr. Castock, in his most impressive style, 'Gentlemen, having by your unmerited kindness, in a manner too flattering to myself, been requested to take this chair to-night —with that entire unanimity and cordiality which has characterised our proceedings from the very commencement, which has not been disturbed by one single divergency of opinion, which is an augury, we trust, of that unbroken happiness which will cement this happy union, which has now been so happily formed for many years.' (Here the chairman, who had been attempting the extemporaneous, evidently returned to his MS. He proceeds) —'Gentlemen, I cordially agreed to the request, so flatteringly made, to officiate as your chairman on this auspicious occasion; and it now becomes my pleasing and agreeable duty to propose for your acceptance the toast of the evening—'The Laird of Drammochdyle and his Bride'—(tremendous and long-protracted cheering). Gentlemen, this is a toast that fortunately requires no recommendation on my part, to ensure its being drunk with the utmost enthusiasm by an attached an grateful tenantry—(hear, hear)—met with the most cordial and unanimous desire to do honour to their highly esteemed landlord, and his lovely—now—partner (enthusiastic cheering).' Here the chairman glanced biographically at the 'happy pair', describing them as 'descended' from long lines of distinguished ancestry'. He concluded by asking the company to 'drink to the toast of the evening with all the honours, and cheers such as the lads of Strathaven can give'. And he added, 'Take the time from me, Mr. Croupier and gentlemen—Hip, hip, hooray'; or, as the *Independent* put it in technical phrase, 'The toast was drunk with nine times nine, and one cheer more, that made the welkin ring—(Band, ''Wooed an' Married an' a''')'.

A great many other toasts were given; and among them were 'The Relatives of the Bride and Bridegroom', which called Dr. Graham to his feet, who, 'in eloquent terms, felicitously acknowledged the toast'; and this operation he repeated, when a big, red whiskered farmer, notoriously known for his profane talk and immoral habits, and who was evidently half-drunk at the time, proposed 'The Clergy of all Denominations', 'which is a class', said the orator, 'which we cannot do without; for they christen oor bairns—(laughter)—when we are born; and as we have see—d from our cheerman's ellygint remarks, can tie the mink— (much laughter)—with a rinnin' k—not—(continued laughter). Gentlemen, the clergy has other mellankollier duties which it would not be right for me to encroach upon, which you all know, as well as me. I can only add that they are patterns to siciety, and ready to give good advice.'—(loud cheers).

Then there was 'Neighbouring Proprietors, and Mr. Crabbice of Vatville', by the Croupier, who delivered himself with considerable originality, and a great amount of rustic vigour, though it may be doubted whether he had that nice descrimination that enables a man to put a point, without any risk of grating on the personal feelings of those he wishes to compliment, inasmuch as when he was approaching the climax in supporting the 'toss', as he pronounced it, he indulged in some personal reminiscences of Mr. Crabbice, with a view to impressing the company with that gentleman's merit, as one who had risen from a very lowly rank, indeed; 'for I've seen him mysel' said the croupier, 'in corduroy

breeks an' a braid bonnet, trudgin' in the road wi's fader's aul'
grey shaltie'. 'And, gentlemen,' said the croupier, changing his
train of illustration, 'if ither proofs were wantin' o' Mr.
Crabbice's deservins, I will tell you an anecdote which occurred
only yesterday. As I was comin' along the Bowl Road, who
should I see but the innkeeper with his spring cart—(laughter)—
coming trottin' doon the gate, which had therein several barrels
and crates peeping out amongst the strae—(much laughter). And
gentlemen, if further testimony were required where oor respected
host had been, here it is which I exhibit. ('The able croupier'
here, 'amid roars of laughter', held up a bottle, off the label of
which he read, 'Genuine whisky. P. Crabbice, Strathaven distillery'.) 'Gentlemen, drink to the landed proprietors and Mr.
Crabbice.' (Band—'For he's a right good fell—low'.)

The editor of the *Strathaven Independent* in his anxiety to do
justice to the occasion by a 'verbatim' report, recorded all this—
translating several words, it is true, into English; though it is probable had he got a little more time for calm reflection as to the
possible effect of these passages on Mr. Crabbice's feelings, he
might have generalised such parts of the croupier's speech under
the phrase 'humorous allusions'; and so reserved 'more space'
for Mr. C.'s elaborate reply which he knew would be judiciously
handed to him in MS for publication, and which he did publish,
but only at the sacrifice of his usual 'Foreign Intelligence'. In it
the proprietor of Vatville expatiated on 'the reciprocal ties
between men in all ranks of life', and 'the responsibility that
devolves upon those in the higher walks to seek the amelioration
of their humbler brethren: consistently with a due regard to that
precious boon of liberty which every subject enjoys under the
glorious constitution of this great empire'.

For Tom Crabbice there was reserved the toast of 'the Ladies',
which came near the end, and afforded scope for the full flow
of that spirited young gentleman's wit, and such a measure of
his slang as he felt it prudent to give. With him the rustics—
many of them 'half seas over' by that time, and others wholly
drunk—laughed consumedly; and when the company soon
thereafter broke up, 'after an evening of the most thorough
enjoyment, which made the fleeting hours pass rapidly on golden
wing' (we quote from the *Independent*)—a few of the would-be
'fast' young farmers sought his congenial company to keep up

the 'spree' for a while longer after the coast was cleared of the 'old fogies'.

Next day George Ross felt terribly out of tune—A day of such scrambling, haste, and pother, followed by a night of drunken uproar, and want of sleep—why the fatigue of a hard day at the joiner's bench was Elysium to this. And as his own comely Kate and her maids clattered about among the dishes that contained the debris of yesterday's feast, trying with what spirit she might in her exhausted state to bring order once more out of chaos, it must be confessed his thoughts were not quite so assured as they had formerly been as to the advantages and amenities of his new position. Only he was not yet fully into 'the set o' the thing', and 'hebit does a grate dale' in that and all such matters.

Chapter XV

A GLIMPSE OR TWO AT AN
UNOBTRUSIVE LIFE

Some two years had come and gone since Robert Morris entered
the employment of Messrs. Patten and Pendicle. The latter
gentleman's increasing infirmities had now laid him aside
altogether from any active share in the business, and Mr. Patten
felt, in a correspondingly weightier measure the responsibility of
filling the place of active partner. At least, he said so. It was not
that he distrusted his clerk, or doubted his efficiency; for what
with his various benevolent schemes and his love of dabbling in
local politics, Mr. Patten not unfrequently quite forgot important
business transactions until reminded of them by Robert Morris,
when he would say, 'Oh yes, by the bye—but I'll leave it in your
hands, Robert, for I've an important meeting to attend just
now'. And he would pull out his big old-fashioned watch from
the waist-band of his breeches, look the time, and returning the
article mentioned to its place, hurry off to take the chair at a
meeting of the Ladies' Mendicant Improvement Society, or to
move a resolution at the annual meeting of the Association for
Vindication of the right of Javanese sailors to wear red waist-
coats.

'But Captain Bullyer, o' the "Happy Return", was jist in,
sir,' the clerk would argue, 'and he wished to have your advice
immediately about the landin' o' the cargo o' oats he has brought
from Archangel.'

'Tut, Robert, go down to the ship and satisfy yourself about
the condition of the cargo, and if it requires to be granaried

directly give the necessary orders. Give the captain my compliments, and tell him I'll be back again before dinner. I'll see him
to-night.'

Mr. Patten held shares in nearly one-half of the vessels belonging to Strathaven, and in the case of several of them, chiefly
traders to the Baltic, he was 'ship's husband', and took charge
of freighting the vessel, and corresponding with the skippers and
agents about the cargoes. Rough and out-spoken enough those
Strathaven skippers were, and some of them, when they came
home off a voyage, would even swear rather fiercely at Mr.
Patten's 'fiddle-faddling'.

'Aye, if Mr. Pendicle had been still at the helm, my lad, it wud
hae been a different tale fae me rinnin' aifter him aboot the cargo.
I never yet turned the Heads comin' hame, but his honest face
was to be seen at the pier-head, gi'en a cheery welcome till his
ship. An' as soon as we neared the jetty, he would jump aboard,
an' gie a hearty grip o' the han' a' roun'; an' as mony questions
aboot hoo we had a' fared. It was like readin' aff the haill log till
him.'

So said Captain Bullyer, when Robert went on board the
'Happy Return' a second time, to say that Mr. Patten would be
down in the course of the afternoon.

'Howsomever, he'll be here whan he comes,' added the skipper, 'an' for bisness, I should say, we'll be better withoot him.
Stap awa' down, my lad, to the cabin, an' I'll gie you a sma'
swatch o' the papers till the men open the hatches, an' syne we'll
tak a vizzy o' the cargo.'

In the cabin the Captain produced his rum bottle, with sundry
accompaniments, and invited Robert to take a 'swig' after his
own example. This invitation was firmly declined—as the
Captain knew from former experience it would be, though he
could not forego the wonted proffer made to everybody indis-
criminately in the dark hole where he had himself drunk and
smoked so often and so long—whereupon followed some 'chaff'
to the effect that were Robert a hundred leagues farther north all
nonsense about eschewing spirits would be knocked out of his
head. Terrible fellows those captains were to drink. Grog would
they swallow almost by the gallon, and their hospitality went
nearly the length of putting it perforce down the throats of those
who were the guests of their cabins. And many stories were told

of respectable Strathaven merchants whom they had entertained after their own fashion, and again set on *terra firma* in a state that made those respectable traders greatly inclined to doubt the fact of the globe being any longer entitled to that designation. Robert in consistency with his principles as a total abstainer had to withstand the boisterous hospitality of his seafaring friends. And the task was less difficult because he had acted on the principle *obsta principiis*, and the skipper, however he might banter could not argue the point. Another companion, however, not seldom took up the question for discussion in an off-hand way.

'I tell ye Robbie man,' James Munro would say, 'it's a' mere haiver that total abstinence business. I never kent a man yet stick rigidly to that principle that hedna some weak and foggy bit in 's head.'

'May be Jamie; but if it leads us to dee richt we maun put up wi the "foggy" bit.'

'But I deny that it leads you to dee richt.'

'It prevents us doin' wrang then.'

'I'm no sure. It acts as an artificial check to prevent a weak, or perverted nature abusin' itsel' by gettin' drunk whenever there is the chance. But what syne—the poor creatur jist turns to some ither sma' vice. It remin's me on John Paterson's riggit coo. The coo had an unco thrawart disposition. For instance, she wudna lose a chance if she got it o' swallowin' the dischclout, an' ance ate body bulk a pair o' drawers belangin' to John 'imsel'; an if she lichtit on a piece horn, or an aul bane, she wud stan' a hail aifterneen wi' her snoot i' the air, champin' at it wi' 'er teeth till she was stiff an' stupit. An' lat John's wife tyce as she wud, the perverse brute wud as soon gie' the livin' teeth fae'er jaws as gi'et up. Syne fan John pat the lave o's his beasts into the aiftermath to feed, the riggit coo was jist as sure to eat inordinately till she got bowden't an' like to split. In fact, John had ance, twice to get the probe an' stick it into her paunch (full swing) to let the fulsome air escape, an' prevent an actual rupture of the ill-conditioned breet's stomach.'

'That surely has little to dee wi' total abstinence.'

'Heely, heely, my freen'. I'm comin' to the point. The riggit coo's "proclivities", to speak properly, became so troublesome to John, that at last he resolved on strong measures, got a pair o' gweed iron branks, an' fan the lave o' the kye war turned into "clover", John took the riggit coo an' tether't her fast on a bare scaup, whaur he was sure she cudna indulge to excess in ony shape fatever; an' as he drave in the baikie emphatically wi's heel, he muttered atween his teeth; "Wae worth, ye beastie, but I'se mak a teetottler o' ye at ance".'

'That's raither poor argument, Jamie.'

'But nane better's require't. Your "scriptural argument", as ye ca't 's no worth a rush. No really sane man will say that the Bible, directly or indirectly, *forbids* the moderate use o' intoxi- catin' drink. No really great physiologist will say that intoxicatin' liquors are necessarily injurious to the healthy subject. Then, as to your "expediency", I admit if ye're a morally weakly charac- ter, there's nae harm in absteenin' personally, but to say your example 's o' mair value *because* you're an abstainer, than mine, who am a moderate drinker, but a temperate man, is jist equiva- lent to sayin' that the example o' John Paterson's riggit coo wi' the branks on is better for the bovine race in general than the example o' the doddit coo, wha only ate her decent fill on the best pasture ye cud pit her on, an syne lay doon to ruminate.'

'Weel, your illustration 's an' odd aneuch ane; only it happens to be rational creatures we're dealin' wi', an' no kye, upon whom the example of the riggit coo an' the doddit wud, I suspect, be much o' a piece.'

'I kenna. Ye speak o' rational creatures. Noo it's jist as such that I appeal to the man, an' call upon him to exercise self-control as a free an' responsible moral agent; you say, "No, no, lat me clap the branks upo' you first".'

'Tut, Jamie, I impose no bondage, but simply say, abstain from what can do no good, an' may do much harm, which has been the ruin o' thousands, an' which the more it is meddled with, from its very nature, maks you the less on your guard as to its dangerous character.'

'That min's me neist upon a temperance lecture I ance heard fan I was an apprentice loon. It was in a toon a lang way to the north o' this they ca' Ehberdeane. I had steppit intil a hall no far fae the principal street o the place, where the Temperance Society, a set o' decent bodies, met weekly, to keep ane anither in coontenance. The same decent mennies, and the same decent wivies, cam up duly weekly on the Friday nicht, an' pat their penny or their bawbee into the plate at the door; the same decent cheerman gae oot the bittie o' a paraphrase to be sung, an' made "remarks" introducing the lecturer and extollin' the "cause". Syne cam the great bisness o' the nicht, a lecture on the subject, with which the decent audience were already brimfu', an' had been for mony a day. It was won'erfu' hoo they cheer't an' "hear, hear't" the "speaker". Weel, the nicht I mention it was a lecturer o' the League, nae less, an' "King Alk-kohol" was sair ta'en through han' I'se assure you. An' to prove the calibre o' the lecturer an' his hearers, the fellow quotit fae Burns the lines in the "Earnest cry and prayer":

> But bring a Scotsman frae his hill,
> Clap in his cheek a Highland gill,
> Say such is royal George's will,
>   An' there's the foe,
> He has nae thought but how to kill
>   Twa at a blow.

"Aye", said the lecturer, resumin', "aye, ma freens' ye see the effeck o' alk-kohol. 'He has nae thocht', 'nae thocht', noo; na, na, that's jist the effecks o' alk-kohol—it taks awa a man's thocht. It prevents his exerceesin' the poo'er o' thocht". An' so on he went, the rampant idiot, so utterly misconceivin' the drift o' the lines as to interpret them as exposin' alochol to opprobrium for the vera effect which would justly claim our admiration, if produced by it, and which these vera lines say it produced.'

'Noo, suppose ye heard a stupid lecture on temperance, what do you inter fae that?'

'That except the audience (beggin' yer pardon, Robbie) had been o' the sort described at the ootset o' oor talk, instead o' cheerin' sic drivel, they wud hae hootit the fellow doon an' sent him back to the mair useful an' legitimate bisness o' mendin' aul' sheen.'

Chapter XVI

MARRIED, AND SETTLED
IN THE COUNTRY

WE seem in some danger of altogether dropping out the principal character in these sketches; which catastrophe must be avoided until the proper time comes, at least. And so to our tale:—

Edward Boyce was, at last 'married, and settled in the country', that fate which a London fashionable of last century is said to have invoked upon a person he disliked as the severest earthly punishment he could think of. Edward expected to find it the perfection of human happiness. And, truth to say, there seemed to be no special reason why his experience should fall greatly short of his expectations. Possessed of competent means, with abundant opportunities of making himself alike useful, respected, and beloved; and above all blessed with the society and confiding love of an intelligent and amiable wife, his cup of earthly enjoyment was surely not very far from running over.

However, we are told, on the highest authority, that a 'man's life consisteth not in the abundance of the things which he possesseth'. And it has been, and we presume ever will be the case that external conditions come to be the means of elevating our life to a higher level or the opposite, just according to the light in which the actuating principles within the man enable him to view them. And they will have their influence the one way or the other. Edward Boyce was a young man of fair ability, and amiable temper; and prior to his father's death it had not occurred to him that he was destined to do otherwise than pursue an arduous professional career. But on that event taking place, his mind, as we have seen had very considerably changed.

Perhaps it was not the wisest course he resolved to adopt; yet if it seemed to present a little prematurely the *otium* of the old Roman, it did not by any means necessarily preclude the enjoyment of the *dignitate* therewith.

'By gor,' said Tom Crabbice, 'if I was only laird of Drammochdyle, with no governor, and no younger brothers, wouldn't I enjoy life?'

And Edward Boyce did not altogether overlook this view of the matter. Fishing and shooting, not very seldom in the company of the young gentleman just named, engaged a considerable part of his time, and when autumn came, the dinner and evening parties at Drammochdyle, came thick and fast. It was their first season, and newly-wedded people, who were expected to lead the 'society' of the neighbourhood, must not grudge a pretty liberal expenditure in this way. Nor did they. And, perhaps, it would be a mistake to say that Mr. and Mrs. Boyce suffered more in the shape of little vexations through occasional failure in the desired effect of these social gatherings, or lassitude in the reaction of a successful 'party', than is the common experience of all who engaged in such matters.

Still, as the months passed on, these things did not suffice quite to fill up the round of life. Only the laird had the management of his property besides. And he would gravely perambulate this and the other corner of his estate in the company of his 'ground officer', Peter Tamson, a grim old crofter, who wore a braid blue bonnet alike to kirk and market, seldom was at the trouble to don a neckerchief, or button his shirt collar, lickit sneeshin immensely, and delivered his opinions with great curtness and emphasis. It was not that the laird had any very profound or exact knowledge of his estate and its conditions; and therefore it was a weakness to pretend to Peter Tamson, at least, that he had. Peter had sair't his father before him, and knew all the outs and ins o't.

'Na, na, Sir,' Peter would say, 'Dinna ye be gow't owre wi' Barreldykes; he's a fair tongue't fleep but hame drauchtit— hame drauchtit.'

'Well, but, Peter, we must give fair encouragement to such an enterprising tenant.'

'Enterprise here, enterprise there, gar him carry oot the condishons o's tack. It's a' ae thank tae ye, wi' him.'

'Oh, but Mr. Castock has done a great deal upon the farm.'

'I ken brawly fat he's deen, an' fat he hasna deen. Luik there, sir, at the half o' the lang mairch ditch atween him and Gouckstyle. He's bun' to scour that stank ilka twa year. An' ye may see fu it's full't wi' the ironeery goor to the vera tap nar han', chokin' up ilka drain that rins in till't, a' because it disna affeck's nain lan'. To my certain k-nowledge, he hisna pitna a spad in't for four years.'

'Well, that should be looked after, Peter.'

'Luikit aifter! Maybe; as gin I hadna yaumer't on about it till I'm hearse. But fat'll ye dee wi' the man that think's he's so far ben wi' the laird that he canna dee wrang?'

And Peter took a severe and ample pinch, glad, no doubt, of the opportunity of speaking a word in season. And thus would the laird and his ground officer discuss and settle matters of detail. Upon questions involving general principles, Edward was wont to consult Mr. Crabbice, senior.

Then there was the particular region of effort in which Mrs. Boyce took an active interest—visiting the poor, getting the bairns schooled, and such like. There was, for example, the family of Jamie Tocher, a ne'er-do-weel labourer, or rather a man who tried every possible dodge to escape honest labour. He had forsaken the pick and spade, and gone after stray jobs, such as droving a few cattle to market, hanging on as assistant hostler about some hostlelry, and paid chiefly in whisky, till kicked about his business. At one time he had hawked stoneware, and at another 'thigged' corn in his own behoof. His slattern wife was a fruitful vine; the family numbered eleven gaunt, hungry bairns, and even *minus* the head of the house, who was understood to be away presently 'raising the wind' in a new speculation, with a crony who possessed a horse and cart, and raffled apples and bought old iron, they were not very easily kept in provender. And as the parental characteristics were strongly marked in every one of the offspring—as the family took the donations of benevolence as their right, and were as ill off after as before—there was likely to be some scope for philanthropy in connection with the Tocher household. Then it so happened that Johnny Duncan took a 'drow', and became for the time an object of special attention. Johnny recovered, and was by and by toddlin' about again, and though for a good many months, by his own account, very weakly, and threatening a 'dropasy', yet the dropsy, too, wore off. Only Mrs. Ellison had fallen upon the ice and was sair daumer't, being an on-freely woman. She required great nursing and much sympathy, and the souter, honest man, had little capacity in that way. He would verily sit gossiping and smoking with his cronies in his dirty, little hut of a shop, till late in the evening, without any special urgency of business, while poor Mrs. Ellison lay grainin' in her easy chair, under the dim light of the black eely lamp, with a wee tablie and one or two decoctions thereon at her elbow.

'Eh na, Mrs. Muggart, he's nae come in yet, an' its half-past nine—lang bed time.'

'That's jist the gate o' them. Fat care they fat folk thole.'

'Deed that's true. For *he*'ll sit there and birsle's shins for an hoor on en', an, thinks himsel' a gane gin he rise i' the mornin' to tak' aff the aise, or fesh in a fraucht o' water. But seerly he's gane up the toon.'

'Na, na, the smith's hearth was black oot an hoor sinsyne, fan' I cam' hame, but the licht's aye burnin' i' the choppie. I'se warran' they'se be there a' thegither, wi' their clamjamfray.'

'Fat road cam' ye, Mrs. Muggart?'

'Ow, doon the loan jist, an' met the lads half-gates up, gaun hame fae the smiddy wi' their plough irons, an' they war gallantin' me that I hed gie'n them a son an' heir.'

'Keep's Mrs. Muggart, it canna be; the leddy was here this verra aifterneen wi' that stoupie o' calf-fit jeel—a-wat I never liket it, but we mauna say that.'

'The leddy! Mrs. Boyce, ye mean? Dear *me*, Mrs. Ellison, ye are gaen oot o't—I've been at Gouckstyle.'

Gouckstyle in a' the earth!

'Gouckstyle—its ten year—year an' day sin' they war marriet an' the goodwife's lichter o' a braw loon!'

Here the tardy souter's foot was heard, and his hand lifted the latch, which broke the thread of this interesting conversation; or to speak correctly, in these days of electrical science, 'disturbed the insulation' of the speakers.

So, as may be seen, a useful field lay before both Mr. and Mrs. Boyce. Yet in the case of neither the one nor the other was there complete satisfaction in the existing order of things. With Mrs. Boyce there had begun to be a vague, undefined fear of some possible unpleasant result from her father's tippling habits. Through the well-meant kindness of her husband, he was a very frequent guest at table in the house of Drammochdyle, and she dreaded to see a repetition of some of those scenes she had witnessed in the privacy of the manse. And the thought of even her husband seeing her father's humiliation gave her many a miserable hour. It never occurred to her that anybody save herself—her bosom friend, Agnes Wilson, who had now left the manse for a governess's situation—and Robert Morris, in whose good faith and secrecy she had implicit confidence, had ever known of, or believed in the possibility of her father getting drunk. Unlucky for her belief that purple, leaden hue over the once fine features—now disfigured with a flabby fulness—alternating with a flush of fierier red, according as strong drink was in active operation or the reverse. Yet 'twas natural enough that this should not betoken to her what it did to even the cursory observer. 'Twere a hard thing surely for a loving daughter to be driven to the conclusion that her father had the look of a drunkard.

Such then was the thorn in Mrs. Boyce's pillow. With Edward Boyce, now that he had in effect settled down as a country gentleman, the question would occasionally come up, especially when he heard of the professional success, now and again, of some old fellow student, whether he ought not after all to have betaken himself to a more active and stirring life; and the more particularly, as he could not always—and especially after an encounter with Peter Tamson—keep down the suspicion that the business of 'managing his property', to which he had addicted himself, had a good deal of the element of fiction in it. Still there was some force in what his Mentor, Mr. Crabbice, Sen., said of the important duties devolving upon country gentlemen, and especially county magistrates, of whom he was now one, his name having been added to the Commission of the Peace. It was doing the State some service to occupy the judicial bench when a poacher needed to be fined, a strolling tinker sent to jail for some petty depredation, or a publican to have his licence certificate adjusted. And, above all, the position was both responsible and honourable, when their honours the Justices took their seats in Quarter Sessions, under the presidency of Sir Joshua Krustie, to hear appeals from innkeepers and others who deemed they had not got justice at the hands of the local Justices. To all such duties as these, for which his legal training so far fitted him, Edward Boyce resolved to apply himself with becoming assiduity.

Chapter XVII

THE MILL INN AND ITS CUSTOMERS

Our last glimpse of our friend, George Ross, occurred when he was making his *debut* somewhat awkwardly as an innkeeper. In due time, he had got settled down in a thoroughly confirmed sort of way to that business. His habits had become so far fixed in the Bonifacian style that it was pretty certain he would never again be good for much else in any other line of life that demanded the rational use of either his brain or his hands.

George, according to his own views of life, ought to have reckoned himself a fortunate man, inasmuch as he had not only achieved matrimonial sucess in the first instance, but now also by the death of his father-in-law, he came into a not inconsiderable inheritance beyond what had become his on his marriage with blooming Kate Reid.

Nor did the Mill Inn want customers of a certain sort. No doubt, the advent of a railway in the locality had long ago put a stop to the running of the old Tallyho coach; which conveyance was wont to change horses there, while the passengers breakfasted within. And from the same cause some dozen of sturdy carriers that made weekly journeys to Strathaven, and put up at the Mill Inn, tippling not a little often, when they 'forgathered'— these had all been compelled to forego their stated visits to the Mill Inn. But a house where liquor is sold has always a certain power of begetting customers for itself. And thus the very fact that the Mill Inn had come to be less frequented by wayfarers and others, whose circumstances made their calls there more or less a legitimate and necessary thing, was its chief recommendation to certain tradesmen of Strathaven who loved to enjoy each other's society over a social glass.

Of these there were two classes. One was known as the 'fore-neen chaps'. They were the more advanced tipplers, who, come what would, must have their 'caulker' of raw whisky and water in the early part of the day; and for that purpose did not hesitate to go to the Mill Inn daily in twos and threes, miscelleneously sorted, together—keeping up, however, as much of the appear-ance of going there to transact business as might be. The other class met only in the evening, to drink toddy, discuss local politics, and be social. And the mode in which the more shame-faced at least of these assembled, was somewhat amusing. A couple of them who had got the day's labours over, would step quietly along the main street of the burgh to a given point, where they would formally, and in sight of the public of Strathaven, bid each other 'good night'. Then they separated. One went straight on along the street with the air of a man who had some little distance to go past the suburbs; but at the Mill Inn he would pull up short, as if a thought had just struck him, and walk quickly in at the front door. The Mill Inn had, too, a back, or rather side door, and by it his companion of five minutes ago would drop in almost at the same moment as himself. He had merely turned down Batter Lane, as if to go home, but in place of seeking his own abode, had diverged to the left at the first opening, and here he now was at the common 'howff'. By and by two or three others would follow, and so the company for the evening was made up. The attempt to disguise their meeting was flimsy enough to be sure, and deceived nobody; yet it salved the tender consciences of the worthies concerned, and so enabled them to sit down with comfort to their evening's 'fuddle', just as the affable conver-sation with the watchman, as he went home about midnight, tended to confirm the belief of this or the other individual of their number that he was *not* visibly groggy—whatever effect it might have on the watchman's private opinion.

One of the most frequent and unfailing visitors at the Mill Inn, was Daniel Lillie, the legal gentleman of whom the reader has already heard a little. Lillie's capacity for swallowing strong drink was indeed something remarkable in its way. He was never known to miss an opportunity, either by night or by day, of having a glass. From being one of the evening bibbers simply, at the Mill Inn, he had long ago joined the ranks of the 'foreneen chaps'; and he even went beyond most of them; for never did a country client call upon him, anent some petty strife with his neighbour, or such like, but he contrived to have a sitting longer or shorter at the Mill Inn, until the wags of Strathaven had come to call it 'Lillie's office'. Yet all this while Lillie was never seen completely drunk; that is to say not drunk and 'incapable' of going on with such business as he had. And Lillie was understood to do a pretty considerable amount of business after a sort. He had the reputation among the country people around Strathaven of being very clever—a reputation which his well known drunken habits rather tended to confirm than otherwise—and this fact brought numbers of pettifogging cases.

When a horse couper sold a faulty horse, for example, the victim of his knavery would go to Lillie in a state of great wrath, and while he more than half suspected that the couper's 'word of honour' relative to the fifty-shilling steed was nought in the way of legal warranty, declared his readiness to 'ware' half the cost of the beast in getting 'amen's o' the scoonrel'. In such case Lillie's was just his man. Though he knew quite well the value the couper set on such documents as a handy medium for lighting his pipe, he would gravely propose writing him a threatening letter, according to the printed form he had, full of hard sounding legal phrases. 'We'll gie 'im a scare at ony rate', Lillie would say; and then he would tell several stories, of how he had 'twisted the beggars' in this and the other instance. And on his client's motion, they would have 'a dram on the heads o't'. And the worthy client would go home in great good humour, avowing that 'we'se gie 'im law to the mast head'. Then Lillie had had a monopoly of Mr. Crabbice's court business—that is defending publicans, who had come under the lash of the law, when such was the generous will of Mr. Crabbice toward a good customer; prosecuting others who bought whisky and failed to pay their accounts for it; and distraining for rent, as often as needful, amongst a number of semi-pauper tenants, that occupied house property belonging to the proprietor of Vatville.

And Lillie was, too, a boon companion, in an unauthenticated way, of Tom Crabbice's. If old Mr. Crabbice valued him for his intimate knowledge of the outs and ins of law 'dodges', and his capacity, when occasion required, of bewildering and bam-

boozling some member of the great unpaid magistracy—a
Baillie, or a J.P.—by a quirk or a quibble, his son esteemed him
no less, after a fashion, for his social qualities. Lillie could sing
a good song and tell a good story; and the more he drank the
better was his companionship—that is to say, if the rest of the
company were advancing step by step with him. He sung more
boisterously, and told stories more vehemently, both songs and
stories increasing in coarseness and obscenity as he proceeded,
according to the natural law in such cases.

When Tom went 'on the loose', then, Lillie was a very common associate. Of course their companionship was not paraded
on the elder Crabbice's notice; indeed the two friends were
modest enough to keep it a good deal secluded from public
observation by meeting ordinarily by themselves, or with mutual
friends under cloud of night, and not very seldom in quarters
where obviously they would not court the popular gaze. When
socially disposed, the Mill Inn was the usual resort.

'Bravo, Lillie', Tom Crabbice would shout when Lillie had
reached a climax in some midnight orgie at the Mill Inn—'Bravo
Lillie—Health and song', and Tom's glass was once more elevated to his lips. 'Br—vo, 'llie—'ll—a-song', would be hiccuped
out by several other young men, Tom Crabbice's companions,
but who did not possess Tom's enviable faculty of getting drunk
without losing the command of his mental or physical faculties.

'Gentlemin, it's past eleyvn!' the landlord might insinuate,
opening the door, and presenting his person half way into the
room.

'Is that a new discovery, Ross?' Lillie would reply. 'Oh aye,
ye smelt that oor liquor was deen, an' Forbes M'Kenzie was
pressin' ye. Gae fetch to me a pint o'—whisky, an' that 'll sattle
Mr. M'Kenzie.'

'But, gentlemin, ye maun be a little quater.'

'Oh aye, oh aye—all right; fill the stoup again,' and of course
the latter order was obeyed.

Chapter XVIII

'AFTER DINNER'—THE MILL INN ACQUIRES A NEW CUSTOMER

George Ross, as landlord of the Mill Inn, had become quite familiarised with the habits of that class of his customers of whom we have last spoken; and their most unruly proceedings now hardly shocked or astonished him in the least, but seemed quite in accordance with the natural order of things. And why should it not be so, for did not the 'custom' of these 'friends' form the staple of his business? True enough, when Tom Crabbice came with his set, there not unfrequently was heavy damage done in the way of broken crystal and battered furniture; but then Mr. Tom was the proprietor's son, and it would never do to present a bill of charges to him for such trifles. Tom, indeed, would have cursed and sworn at mine host if he had; and might even have taken, as well as vowed vengeance, reckless of whatever retaliation might have been attempted—for Tom knew that George Ross had secrets relative to his private habits which it would have been inconvenient for him to have had revealed; but Tom's was one of those imperious tempers that trust a good deal in such matters to the sheer power of browbeating an inferior.

Well, however, as George Ross was accustomed to Tom Crabbice's disorderly nocturnal proceedings, he was rather surprised on a certain night, when, on going himself to open the door near midnight, at the well known sounds of Tom and Lillie, he heard outside a third voice familiar to him, but not as that of a midnight reveller. Could it be that his ear deceived him? George paused as he undid the door bolts—and sure enough there was

Lillie, with a drunken jeer repeating the very name he had been startled to think of.

'Mr. Boyce, I say, are you a muff? Confound it, as if I were not a married man myself; or have been, which is all the same. Come, come, let's have a tumbler of Ross's real Strathaven; then we'll let you off, and Tom and I will sing—

"We won't go home till morning."

Won't we, Tommy, my boy? Aye, aye, we know the outs and ins of this old village by night as well as by day.'

'Hold your jaw, Lillie,' was the polite rejoinder of Tom Crabbice.

'And many's the sore affront I get with you, my son,' answered the worthy limb of the law as they passed in, Lillie hanging on to the arm of the third person whom George Ross now saw clearly to be Edward Boyce, not staggering, certainly, but evidently flushed with drink.

How Edward Boyce came to be with his present companions at such a time is not long to tell. Both he and Tom Crabbice, with whose close companionship he was still favoured, had been at Captain Ryrie's, at 'the Grove', as the captain styled his residence. Captain Ryrie, as a bachelor, invited only gentlemen on such occasions, and, therefore, Mrs. Boyce had not been along with her husband. The captain's parties, moreover, were always 'jolly'—for he was a connoisseur in wines, as his nose unmistakeably testified—and he had a 'capital cellar'. So, when the dinner party broke up, it was a natural enough sequence, that Tom Crabbice should be in a condition rather to prolong the spree. Seizing Edward Boyce's arm he declared it to be his intention to walk home with him; but it soon became pretty evident that he had at least no particular intention of taking the most direct route to Drammochdyle. Straight down to the centre of Strathaven he went, first turned into one bye street, and then into another, while Edward Boyce, who was considerably under the influence of Captain Ryrie's 'crusted port', walked on little observant of their course, and talking freely and rather unconnectedly. Just as they were emerging again upon the High Street, they met Lillie, who with a good deal of gusto, informed them that he had been at an oyster supper with certain 'fogies' who were thus repaying him for work done. He declared repeatedly his delight at meeting Mr. Boyce under such auspicious circumstances; and at once proposed that they should go into the Mill Inn, which they were just approaching as they walked along. And it was in answer to Mr. Boyce's rather vague remonstrance against this proposal—which Tom Crabbice had practically followed up by rudely battering the door with his stick—that the remarks already given were made.

The three companions were soon seated in the bar parlour; and whisky, with the other materials for making toddy, set on the table by Lillie's order.

'A pipe now, Rossie—confound you, give us a pipe,' said Lillie, as he settled himself down in an old easy chair, which he had pushed up to the table, and began to mix his toddy. 'Now for it gentlemen—the man who can't enjoy a good glass of toddy deserves to be hung, say I. Let me help you to some hot water, Mr. Boyce.'

'Thank you, no. Well, I'll just try one glass,' said Mr. Boyce, with the air of one not quite at home in the circumstances.

Tom Crabbice, after swallowing half a glass of spirits, had sat down with outstretched limbs on a leather covered couch at one side of the room to smoke a clay pipe. Lillie meanwhile addressed himself with considerable ardour to the toddy jug, employing the intervals in filling another pipe.

'Say, now, Mr. Boyce, isn't a glass of toddy a rare good thing after supper. It's what I call a social drink. Here's t'ye Mr. Boyce. Come, sir, mix up a drop.'

'I'm doing very well.'

'Ah, there's a knack in making toddy the right thing. A couple of good glasses of whisky, a fairish nugget of best lump sugar, and as much hot—thoroughly hot water, as fill the tumbler to half an inch from the brim. I fear, sir you're making a wishy-washy mixture there.'

'No; its very good.'

'Too whitish; too whitish. Look at that. There's the real cheery stuff, with the fine mellow golden tinge, an' the smoke curlin' up as ye stir't. But, come sir; you're not tasting at all—my tumbler's three-fourth's empty. Here's to our better acquaintance.'

'Come now, Lillie, give up that nonsense; blow out your pipe and sing us a stave with that cracked voice of yours,' said Tom Crabbice.

'Not now, Tom; not now' interposed Edward Boyce, 'It would disturb the house at this late hour, would it not?'

'I should just like to hear that it did,' answered Tom with a loud laugh. 'A bright idea, truly, for a publican to be disturbed—go a-head Lillie with "Johnny's Grey Breeks".'

Lillie did as desired. And at the close of his song the remnant of his first tumbler quickly disappeared down the singer's throat. Somewhat to Edward Boyce's surprise, he immediately proceeded to fill up again.

'But, gentlemen, we must be going; it's past twelve o'clock,' said Edward, who still manifested symptoms of being somewhat ill at ease.

'Aye, so we shall,' answered Tom Crabbice, who had risen to his legs, and was now smoking in the centre of the floor, 'But first let's have a specimen of Lillie's mimetic powers. You didn't know that Lillie was a mimic? Then you have a rare treat before you. Why, with all his vices, he's the greatest genius out in that line. He'll mimic you any man you like to name, from the parson —beg your pardon Mr. Boyce—or Sir Joshua Krustie, down to Captain Ryrie, or Billy Patten, of Patten and Pendicle.'

It was agreed accordingly that Captain Ryrie should be hit off, and Lillie, who had been industriously mixing and drinking toddy all the while, having set himself properly, mimicked the peculiar, and rather uncouth manner, of the undistinguished and somewhat obtuse warrior so closely, and with such ludicrous effect, that Edward Boyce, notwithstanding a dim notion of the extreme impropriety of his presence in such a place, at such an hour, was not indisposed to wait a little longer to see Lillie come out in one or two other characters. And to beguile the intervals needed by Lillie for 'breathing', he too joined Tom Crabbice in a fresh tumbler of toddy.

Chapter XIX

THE MANSION HOUSE OF
DRAMMOCHDYLE—A HOME SCENE

At the period at which we have now arrived, Edward Boyce had been married about four years, and was the father of two pretty little daughters; one but a year old, the other almost three. He loved his wife and his children, and his life which had passed uneventfully along, had been on the whole a tolerably happy one. Possibly the thought might occur to him occasionally that a little more in the shape of active employment would not be exactly a bad thing even for a laird who managed his own estate (with the aid of his ground-officer in one direction, and his experienced friend Mr. Crabbice, senior, in another)—and who understood himself to be tilling his home farm in such an improved style as to be a sort of model to his tenantry, only that his intelligent 'grieve's' balance sheet—if he had produced one—which he didn't do, not being asked, indeed, would have shown that while great 'results' were produced in crops and cattle, there was no free surplus in name of rent; which would hardly have done with the tenants. Yet things were going on decently with the laird. Doubtless in his home-life there was, quite enough of the conventionally 'social', as distinguished from the strictly domestic element, but that is no uncommon thing with people who have some vacant time and no great superfluity of internal mental resources. He visited much, and was visited in turn by numbers of remarkably agreeable people, who were sufficiently polite to make none of their censorious remarks otherwise than behind his back. At his 'parties', the laird had been known to get hilarious

80

in a high degree toward the close, and jovial even, among the gentlemen, his neighbours. The dinner at Captain Ryrie's and its sequence, was a step farther than before however, and accordingly, on the morrow morning, an uncomfortable stomach, and splitting headache, added emphasis, it must be owned, to Edward Boyce's reflections: and his matured conclusion was that George Ross's whisky toddy required a little practice ere it could be innocuously indulged in.

'Edward, my dear,' said his wife as they sat at breakfast, 'Do eat a little; you take nothing'; and her words broke a constrained silence that had prevailed for several minutes.

'No, thank you; I can't to-day,' was the laird's reply, as he averted his eyes and pretended to see something interesting from the window.

'Have you a headache, dear? Your brow is flushed.'

'Yes; a little. Nothing to speak of. It'll be all right when I get outside to see the overseer at the farm.'

'But Edward,' continued Mrs. Boyce, with an effort more evident than successful to speak in a tone of easy raillery, 'you must take care of that terrible man, Captain Ryrie; he kept you very late last night!'

'Pooh, nonsense, my dear. I was home soon after twelve, and you know it takes half an hour to walk from the Grove.'

But Edward Boyce had not been home till after one o'clock; and his wife could not so readily get over the impression of that alarm which his unexpectedly late stay while absent, and that anguish which his unmistakeably drunken appearance when he arrived, had caused her. She had prudently said nothing at the time, but was now resolved to make a wife's earnest appeal to the better nature of her husband.

'Oh, Edward, if you but knew what weary hours they were that I passed watching for your return.'

'Bless me, Elsie, what a fuss you make,' replied he, in a half irritated tone, 'couldn't you have gone quietly to bed, now, and not been bothering in that way.'

'I cannot bear to think of your absence late at night, dearest Edward.'

'Tuts—do you think I'm not able to take care of myself? D'ye think Captain Ryrie's guests get so jolly that they're not able to find their way home?'

'No, my dear—but—'

'But—you mean to say I was tipsy last night?'

'Edward, how can you be so cruel. But when one is in company with Captain Ryrie and Tom Crabbice, it is not easy to break off in season.'

'Ah, just so; and you don't think I can look after myself as well as Tom Crabbice,' said the laird, evidently losing his temper somewhat.

'I know you can; but, dear Edward, I'm afraid—'

'Afraid we'll both tumble into the ditch together some night. Indeed! Well, when we do, it will only be after the example of a reverend gentleman not unknown to both of us.'

Edward Boyce left the room as he uttered those words, the harshest, by a long way, his wife had ever yet heard from his lips. He strode out to his farm in not the most pleasant frame of mind, nor with the most placid conscience. Yet what could he do but get angry—there was not enough of the true man in him to force from him honest acknowledgement of the mean rascality of his conduct. His poor wife burst into tears. It was a cruel thrust; the first real unkindness from the husband of her love. Had she now fairly sounded and seen the bottom of *his* love and affection? Alas, it was 'an ower true tale' of her father which she had striven to persuade herself was not known to others in the light in which it forced itself upon her. But that it should be cast in her face in its worst aspect by him for whom her love was stronger than life itself, as true love ever is, whose welfare she so sincerely sought, and upon whom she would so fondly have leant for counsel and support!

That very night there was a 'party' at Drammochdyle, and Mrs. Boyce, with whatever sinking of heart, had to welcome her guests, including Captain Ryrie, Tom Crabbice, and sundry of their special friends, with 'nods and becks and wreathed smiles'. The laird, partly it might be to drown the unwelcome recollection of his own part in the morning scene, had become uncommonly gracious to her above all others in the early part of the evening. In the latter part, too, he got quite as jolly, as usual; and when his guests retired, at once collapsed from a state of boisterous hilarity, to something verging on silent sulkiness.

Chapter XX

'FRIENDS IN COUNCIL'

Edward Boyce's first visit at the Mill Inn was by no means the last. We do not mean to describe minutely the how or why of any one or more of his nocturnal excursions thither. Perhaps he seldom, if ever, left Drammochdyle to go there of set purpose; and of one thing he felt very certain—that it was *not* for the love of strong drink that he went to the Inn. He indeed rather affected to be altogether above the style of tippling indulged in there. But Tom Crabbice was irresistible when one had nothing particular on hand to engross his attention, and Lillie, slightly rakish as he was, and rather below the mark as a companion, had such rare social qualities. And then there were, too, a few others, fellows of infinite humour, who dropped in to the Mill Inn at odd hours of an evening. Yes, it *was* 'love of the company', and nought else, that led Edward Boyce to the Mill Inn.

Well, we have no wish really to dispute about the distinction. 'Tis often enough made, at least, and we grudge no man the benefit of what he deems the more euphonious reason for frequenting the public house, or seeking the social board at which strong drink is an essential element of the good fellowship to be obtained. If in either case the result be the same, and a moderate amount of observation would tend to establish us in the belief that such is the rule—confirmed, it is true, by some exceptions—we need not fight over a strict verbal definition of the motives that impelled thereto.

Poor Mrs. Boyce saw only too clearly whither matters were tending. She had never again ventured to attempt remonstrance or entreaty with her husband. His conduct towards her, except when under the influence of drink, or suffering from the reaction of over indulgence in that way—in which phase of human exist- ence a man is pretty nearly the most contemptible as well as the most miserable object in the universe—was on the whole kind, though but fitfully so. Yet as she thought once and again of anew appealing to him, the terrible rebuff that to get tipsy was but following the example of her father always rose before her, and sealed her lips, and wrung her heart in many an hour of bitter anguish.

To only one friend had she ventured to open her mind on the subject. And that was her old companion, Agnes Wilson, who now occupied the situation of governess in a gentleman's family in the north of England. Agnes, after an absence of two or three years from Strathaven, had consented, at the invitation of Mr. and Mrs. Boyce, to spend the summer holidays at Drammoch- dyle. She had not failed to observe with pain the change in Edward Boyce's habits, and therefore it was hardly a surprise to her when Mrs. Boyce revealed the sad tale of her husband's growing neglect of his home and family, and his increasing dissi- pation, and how all this was embittered by the thought that, as her father's physical strength declined, so did his power to resist the influence and conceal the effects of *his* habits.

'What shall I do, Agnes—what would I not do to save Edward from this infatuation?' exclaimed Mrs. Boyce in tones of anguish. 'Oh could I but keep him from being out at night with Tom Crabbice, and his companions all might yet be well.'

Agnes Wilson was at a loss for a reply. She knew quite well the character of Tom Crabbice, and guessed not inaccurately of the baleful influence he had exercised on Edward Boyce; but at the same time she had seen with pain an unmistakeable attach- ment, as she believed, on Mr. Boyce's part to strong drink for its own sake. And she had also heard it hinted, in other circles, that Mr. Boyce was giving way to habits of dissipation, that he was known to frequent the Mill Inn with companions suitable in no respect for him; and whose leading characteristic, to use their own phrase was a liking for 'the company'—or speaking plainly, and quite as accurately, the vulgar and debased habit of tippling. Nay, 'twas even whispered, that he and Dr. Graham, his father- in-law, had come to high words together in their cups, with none to witness the scene save his own servants, the cause of quarrel being something which neither of them could clearly make out when again quite sober. Agnes felt that conscientiously—and specially as a believer in total abstinence, she could only reply— 'It is not enough, Elsie. The evil you dread must be cut at the root, and not only in the branches.'

'And how can that be, Agnes?'

'I know but of one way, Elsie, that is perfectly open to all who feel this temptation, and perfectly sure in its results.'

'And what is that?'

'It is to forswear that drink, which brings so many to misery and premature death, and steeps so many in crime.'

'Alas, my dear, you only mock me,' said Mrs. Boyce, covering her face with her hands. After a minute of silence, she added, 'Ah, Agnes, do you recollect our discussions long ago on that subject, when Robert Morris was a poor lame lad living with his mother. Surely, surely he was right though father and ourselves, and everybody called him a fanatic—no you didn't, Agnes—but everybody else. And how angry all his friends were when he refused to become Mr. Crabbice's tenant at the Mill Inn where his companion, George Ross, now is; but how different from the handsome young joiner—a rude, red faced publican. And how different Robert Morris is too!'

'Different from what he was,' inquired Agnes Wilson, with an eager glance at her friend. 'And has he too'—

'I forgot, Agnes, that you have not seen Robert for three years. He is different yet so like what he was long ago.'

'Is he still Mr. Patten's clerk?'

'Not his clerk, Agnes; his partner now.'

'His partner!'

'Yes, dear Aggie; there is a progress upward or downward with us all it seems. And so when Mr. Pendicle died last year, Mr. Patten and all the friends were so much pleased with Robert's faithful management of the business that they made him junior partner. But I wish to go and consult Mr. Morris—no let us still call him Robert Morris—about another matter.' And Mrs. Boyce added in a tone of affected cheerfulness 'so you must go with me, Agnes, and renew your acquaintance with him, if a man so engrossed with freights and ledgers has any time left for the talk of silly women.'

'The worse luck to his freights and ledgers if he has not!' was Agnes's-half comic, half-serious reply. 'We shall go whenever it is convenient for you.'

Chapter XXI

THE ETHICS OF LOVE AND COURTSHIP

The attentive reader of this history will probably remember that one of the characters therein—James Munro to wit—was wont to hold stout debate with Robert Morris, *de omnibus rebus*; and the two would take to different sides in the argument, if it were only for argument's sake. Early on a given summer evening they had met as usual, and the subject of their talk was love and courtship. A farmer in the vicinity had courted and won a blooming damsel, whose father was also a careful agriculturist in the Strathaven locality. The match was considered eligible by the relatives on either side, and the preliminaries were just being settled, when the bridegroom expectant found that the tocher which his prospective father-in-law was prepared to pay down fell well nigh fifty pounds below his anticipations. 'That's hardly aneuch, Mains,' quoth the prudent young man, 'ye gied Kirsty, 'er aul'est sister, a score o' notes mair, didna ye—an' a better plenishin' forbye?' 'Ye better jist be takin't noo Sawney, an' mak nae words aboot fat Kirsty gat.' 'Na, na; ''fair play's a jewel'',' and so they came to high words. Mains declared that he should 'dee wi' his ain as he liket, as lang's *his* heed was abeen the grun', and Sawney replied—'Ye may keep yer gear till ye dee, man; there's mair women i' the wardle nor *your* dother'—and so they parted. The maiden, in connection with whom the controversy arose, 'grat', it was said, on learning the fact that her lover was off for good. In a month thereafter, having been duly 'cried on', he was married to the daughter of another man, who dealt in cattle, and was said to have been working on Sawney's tender feelings previous to the rupture described, by not obscurely hinting at the 'wechty moggin' that the man who took his dawtit Meg, his only bairn, would obtain. So Meg became Sawney's bride, albeit she was 'gleyed' of an eye, and had a beard almost an inch long. But she was a muscular woman, and fit for a deal of hard work. Mains, in a fury, raised an action for breach of promise before the Sheriff. Only it came to nothing. Sawney was not so unwise as to have ever written letters of an affectionate character to any young woman. And the only evidence against him was intangible gossip, save the testimony of Mains's servant girl, who heard Sawney, after calling his 'umquhile' sweetheart to the door on a certain occasion, when she happened to be busy baking oat bannocks, say—'Fu mony fowk are *ye* gaun to seek, Tibby? I'm only haein' my ain sister an' breeder, an' Tam Unerson, an' some ane by wye o' maiden; it's a rael herrial to seek a maingye o' fowk.' And so the action fell.

This is an unreasonable digression, only the circumstances gave rise to the conversation following.

'Speak o' the nobility an' gentry sacrificin' the feelings o' their daughters, an' sons too, in order to effect advantageous matches,' said James Munro. 'I tell ye what it is, Robbie, there's not a more heartless set in that respect than just the class of well-to-do farmers.'

'But observe ye, Jamie; ye cannot plant true affection where the very elements o't dinna exist. It's not six months since Mains's Tibby cam through this ordeal, an' yet ye say Tibby smirks an' smiles as blithely as ever, and is settin' her cap at the wealthy widower owre the knowe.'

'Just so; an' why not? She's been taught from infancy to regard a ''gweed bargain'', in the light o' a man wi' money, an' a well stocked farm—that solely and simply—mental an' moral qualities go for nothing; they don't count at all. A'ye can say is, that Tibby 's been an apt an' ductile pupil o' the system under which she has been trained. And so it is as a rule—the young women are quite as heartless as the men, an' give in to the prevailin' order o' things cheerfully.'

Robert Morris shook his head, and smiled as he answered, 'Jamie, Jamie, dinna add ungallantry to yer cynicism.'

'Neither I do; I speak accordin' to the facts.'

'So you aver that among the class o' people who make

''prudent'' matches, there is rarely any true affection, even on the woman's side.'

'Not that exactly. Only when ''prudence'' comes to be a guidin' motive, I wud be inclined to mislippen the depth as well as genuineness o' the affection on either side; while I am bound to say, on the other hand, that there is not unfrequently a sentimentalism professed which discards common sense considerations in connection with the object of regard or *dis*regard as the case may be, and which, as bearing upon true and well-founded love, is equally worthless. And in this sort of heartless sentimentalism women, pretending, it may be, to some refinement, indulge at least as much as men.'

'Jamie, have a care o' yer tongue! You'll bring down on your head the vengeance of the whole sex.'

'Stay—ye havena heard the extent o' my heresy yet. We have been speakin' o' mercenary matches. Of course in a case like that of Mains's daughter, we reckon Sawney a pitiable an' contemptible sort of blockhead; but we can hardly even mak' the pretence of feelin' for Tibby, because if she gets the widower—though she'll hae her ain a-dees wi' his half-score o' ill bred geets—she'll just be as weel content as if she had got Sawney. Absurd to think o' a gnawing life-long heartache for her—a dreary, desolate void in her heart of hearts, which human sympathy dare never approach—all because of one once so dear to her—perhaps as dear to another now—but when we see a case of what seems fair and honourable love, where the man from whim, or heartlessness, deserts the woman he has led to trust in him, we denounce him as a villain and very justly say I. He has committed a most cruel and heartless offence, and which may entail life agony on another; but how comes it that we pass so slightly over the case of a woman who acts similarly toward the man whose attentions she has encouraged, and whose affections she has thus gained; and such cases are at least as common on the part of women as of men?'

'Weel, ye know men are not supposed to be so touched with those tender feelings. They have mair mental stamina mair o' the ''stalk o' carl hemp'', as Burns says, and feel it less, perhaps.'

'Feel it less, Robert!' said James Munro, starting to his feet, 'You've got that length only yet. Let me tell you, my boy, that a true man, who has given his affections to a woman, sincerely

and honestly, and who in place of the honourable return of constant affection he had reason to expect, finds himself deserted—
be it from caprice, or superficial sentimentalism, or some grovel-
ling motive—suffers, and cannot choose but suffer, an agony of
heart and spirit more than it is in a woman's very nature and
mental constitution to realise or be capable of bearing—suffering
deeper and stronger than she *can* know! Yet bear it he must in
silence, unpitied, probably laughed at.'

'Jamie,' said Robert Morris, stretching himself quietly back
on his seat, and eyeing his companion, 'ye're gettin' eloquent.
I've heard it said, that when a dull man even, speaks the real and
deepest feelings of his heart, he will rise to eloquence. Is it too
much to make a personal application to the speaker in this case?'

'Let the ''personal application'' come anither time, Robbie.
Here's your sister'; and James went toward the opened door.
'Lizzie,' he said, unceremoniously seizing her hands and grasping them firmly in his own, 'I've been libelling the sex to which
you belong, as inconstant and shallow sentimentalists.'

'And do you believe that?' was the laughing rejoinder.'

'I'll require evidence, at least, to make me disbelieve it.'

'And yet you surely will not deny us the poet's meed of
praise—

> Oh, woman, in our hours of ease
>   Uncertain, coy, and ill to please;
> When pain and anguish wring the brow,
>   A ministering angel thou.'

'Well, perhaps not,' said James, slowly quitting his hold. 'But
that was not exactly the question. Robert, who professes to be
a sort of minor Plato on this subject, will understand that aspect
of it—the aspect of pure philanthropy and friendship—better.'

'Well, a couple o' ladies from Drammochdyle are with my
mother, an' want to see the ''minor Plato!''' said Lizzie.

Chapter XXII

DIFFERENT YET SO LIKE

'He is different, yet so like what he was long ago.' So said Mrs. Boyce of our friend Robert Morris, and so thought Agnes Wilson when again introduced to Robert. The same quiet, unpretending manner was still there, but now with somewhat more in it, perhaps, of the self-possession of a man accustomed to mix in general society, to meet business people on their own level, and to avoid meeting *un*business people when anything of more importance has to be done. Robert's greeting of his old friend was one of the most cordial kind. He *was* heartily glad to see Agnes Wilson, and as was use and wont with him, he did not fail to express it in word and manner. Possibly a man more accomplished in what passes for 'politeness' with a good many people in these days, would have gone through the thing with much greater propriety; talking over a good deal of namby-pambyism in well-set phrases, carefully avoiding the utterance of a single sentence which could be mistaken for plain common sense, and rising vastly superior to the petty facts of everyday life, and the small and vulgar people who pay the least attention to these. But this was not natural to him; nor had his experience in the world quite led him to believe that human life was meant to be a sort of genteel comedy, the actors in which are bound to be *so* plausible, *so* accommodating, that truth must give place to convention; and honest feeling to an assumed and skin-deep 'gentility'. And so it was that Robert Morris, finding Mrs. Boyce desirous of talking on some business matters with him, at once proposed to introduce to Agnes his friend, 'Jamie Munro', assuring her that he was a hard-headed, honest fellow; as clever a mechanic as he was an intelligent, outspoken companion. 'An' if ye dinna quarrel over some debateable point, I'm sure h'll keep you an' Lizzie in matter for argument till we rejoin you.'

Agnes was taken to the small room where James was, and which Robert called specially his own, and introduced accordingly, while Robert remained with Mrs. Boyce in the parlour for discussion of private business matters.

The mood of James's mind at the time was a little peculiar. The subject of discussion between him and Robert has been already indicated. In his ardent impulsive way, James had been accustomed to maintain that, among mundane forces, man's will was the supreme power; that over woman's nature specially it was meant to rule; and thus, in the relations between the two, as regards the tender affections, a man could, if he chose, all but *command* the love of any woman. Perhaps his recent experience had somewhat rudely disturbed some of his theorisings in this direction. And in his solitary musings and *general* disquisitions, he was just then disposed to lay quite as much emphasis on the moral deflections of woman's nature as upon her intellectual inferiority. Yet, *in the presence* of a true and *sensible* woman, James felt his philosophy desert him sadly. After all, here was a fit and worthy companion; and the strong feeling so near a-kin to reverence, which may be no part of the more refined, sentimental affection, but which lies so near the root of true and lasting love— the love that in itself embodies the principle of self-sacrifice for the object of regard, as the one vital element without which it were mere selfishness and not love—*this* feeling James found still to have its place within him; and his cynicism broke down under the thought that, after all, there must be—aye that there were— women capable of true and lasting love.

In a brief 'confab' with Agnes Wilson and Lizzie Morris, he rattled away much in his usual style. James was only a plain working mechanic, and he could not but feel that the fact of Agnes Wilson having lived in more refined circles than those he had been wont to mingle in, gave her certain advantages which he possessed not. He had sufficient confidence in himself, however, to believe that his homely manners, and direct yet not disrespectful modes of speech, ought not to be offensive to any whose good opinion was worth having. And so, on Lizzie Morris reviving the topic touched on in the close of last chapter, by rallying James on his lack of proper and chivalrous feeling, and asking the aid of Agnes to shame him into a better mind, he had gone right into a somewhat vague but none less emphatic defence of his position. His reasonings on the subject we shall not here repeat.

In the meanwhile, Mrs. Boyce discussed her business matters with Robert Morris in another room. What these were need not be specially dwelt upon. It was not the first occasion on which the poor lady had called upon him for advice in relation to her father's pecuniary affairs which had got involved to a serious extent; inasmuch as Mr. Crabbice, sen., now held a bond from him, in virtue of which, partly from Dr. Graham's ignorance of business transactions, and partly from the shame and reluctance he felt at consulting any one better acquainted with such things than himself, the generous proprietor of Vatville was able to extract usorious interest, whilst he pretended to favour, and sympathise in the difficulties of his victim. This subject Mrs. Boyce dared not to speak of to her own husband, but she had told it to Robert Morris; told how it preyed on her father's mind, and made him miserable and ill. She was not now a little comforted by the assurance from Robert who had pondered over the matter in all its bearings, that he was beginning to see his way to a remedy.

'But you'll visit us again, Miss Agnes, before you leave' said Mrs. Morris as the ladies were about to leave.

'Perhaps I may; but my time is short.'

'And how kind of you to think of us in your grand English home; and to mind on all my family so well.'

'Oh, Mrs. Morris' said Agnes laughingly, 'you must not suppose that a poor governess can get so exalted as to find it needful to forget all her old friends. You may trust to my calling on you unbidden even when I next come back.'

Chapter XXIII

A DEATH BY 'APOPLEXY'—
DR. GRAHAM GONE FOR EVER

'THE parson of Strathaven dead! You don't mean to say so, Ross! Then we shan't see Boyce here to night—He's old Graham's son-in-law d'ye see.'

The speaker was Daniel Lillie: the person he addressed directly mine host of the Mill Inn; and two persons were present besides in that hostelry, to whom the latter part of his remarks were less directly addressed. Two 'friends' of Mr. Lillie, in short. One was a seedy-looking person, with a cadaverous countenance of seemingly the same profession as Lillie himself; the other of stouter proportions, wore a good deal of the aspect of a Baltic skipper who had not been in active employment afloat for some considerable time.

'An' what did old Graham die of Ross?'

'Apoplexy, I believe. So the postman says. He fuish the news comin' in fae his roon this forenoon.'

'Apoplexy! Well I've heard that he's been goin' intilt stunnin' for a while, parson as he was. Last time he was at Drammochdyle, and that's nae lang ago he got bleezin' aifter dinner.'

'Aye, he's been vera hard o' the bottle for some time. Faimily affairs had been vexin' him it's said.'

'Faimily affairs!' exclaimed Lillie. 'How? He has no family but a daughter married to one of the best fellows out in these degenerate days—Edward Boyce.'

'Aye, but ye see they've no been 'greein' that sair for sometime. This is November, an' I b'lieve as lang back as Lammasday there had been some quarrelin'. An' Johnnie Duncan, the beadle, the vera last time he wus in here wus tellin' me, he suspeckit there wus something agley atween the Crabbices an' the doctor, as weel. For Tom had been up at the Manse, an' wus clositit wi'm in's ain study for a while, an' there wus some heich words. An' Tom wus deman'in' money, for, says he, "ye've drucken lang aneuch gratis." So ane o' the lasses taul Johnnie— she happen't to be i' the passage at the time, ye see, an' overheard them. An' Tom, threaten't till inform Edward Boyce aboot it which set the doctor fair mad—for he wus aye a heich-spirited man, ye ken. An' it en'it at that time in the doctor makin' owre to Tom Crabbice, b' wye o' sale on the pretence that it didna fit him, o' the fine fleet powney that he got in a present fae the pairish aboot twa years sin syne. For ye min' we war a' speakin' aboot it in this vera house at the time; an' Tom swoor it wus a perfect moddle o' a powney, an' worth sixty poun, gin' it wus worth a groat.'

'Aye, aye; I'see, I'see,' answered Lillie, who had been nodding now and again significantly, during the time George Ross was speaking, 'Tom's aye Tom. Give the devil his due and we'll know where—some folks will land.' The latter part of the sentence was possibly a modification, and Lillie, whose appearance was now visibly more debauched than when he was first introduced in this story, continued with a slightly thoughtful air— 'Well, I'm very sorry to hear of Arthur Graham's death. 'Pon' my word, he had a rare head on his shoulders. At College he was the first man in everything: an' a better hearted fellow never lived. He was a gran' scholar. As a parson, he was, perhaps, of late times, a little free as the world wags, but he's gone, Bless me!' And Lillie turned his eyes to the corner of the ceiling and mused.

'I'm taul'' said George Ross, after a somewhat awkward pause, 'that on comin' in fae sermon, on a Sunday, aifter denner, he wud sit doon 'imleen an' finish half-a-dizzen gless o' raw whusky withoot stirrin' fae his seat. Noo that wus dangerous in a man wi' his full hebbit o' body, ye ken.'

'So poor Dr. Graham's gone. Well, well, it's the way with us all,' said Lillie, abruptly, and breaking off his reverie, though still speaking, as if merely thinking aloud. 'But luik smart, noo, Ross, an' bring in three donallies here. I expeckit to see Mr. Boyce, an' introduce him to my freens, Captain Bulkhead and Mr.

Tipperty; but that canna be, and in the circumstances it would be highly disrespectfu' to think o' makin' an evenin' o' it by oorsells. Quick.'

'Yes, sir.'

And so the 'donallies' were brought in and paid for in fractional silver coins, hunted out of the lower depths of Lillie's trousers pocket, and put down with an impressive promptitude and gravity. The liquor was devoted 'to the memory of Dr. Graham—drunk in solemn silence.' The quantity, however, was absurdly and provokingly small in the case of three well trained tipplers, who had met in anticipation of a regular and business-like set-to, to finish the day with. Lillie sat and uttered one or two sounds, something between a cough and a groan; he found that his hand was very reluctant to part company with the diminutive donallie; and, respect for the departed notwithstanding, a couplet came into his mind with such force as almost to reach his lips, which runs in this wise:

> The four-gill chap we'se gar him clatter,
> An' kirs'en him wi' reekin' water.

To have uttered it, would have been too broad a hint to Captain Bulkhead, yet Lillie had an intense desire at the moment to test the extent of the Captain's generosity, or rather, perhaps, to test the extent of his financial resources; he knew Mr. Tipperty to be 'clean', as usual with that gentleman. So he sat, groaned again, lifted his glass and looked at it, and then broke in, 'Ross, gie's a draw o' yer pipe afore we go.'

The landlord complied, and Lillie, putting one leg over the other, leant back for a silent, deliberate smoke. This was throwing Bulkhead and Tipperty on their own resources. The latter had been so well sucked out, mentally and physically, as well as pecuniarily, that he could sit still under any circumstances (except the pressure became so severe as actually to lacerate his skin and break his bones), with perfect composure. Moreover, he at once guessed the significance of Lillie's smoke, and cordially fell in with his humour. Bulkhead had a considerable remnant of a sort of vague physical energy still in him. And to sit there with two utterly silent men, who only grunted occasionally, and at intervals jingled their empty glasses—quite accidentally—

was very irksome; his sole mental exercise, at any time, being 'jaw' about things within the compass of his understanding, and his prime recreation to mix and drink toddy. Twenty minutes of this, and still no sign from the Captain but an uneasy 'hirstling' about upon his seat, and an alternation between purple and green upon his countenance, was surely proof positive that the honest man really had not the coin in his pocket to pay for 'half a mutchkin'; and Lillie, not unaccustomed to weigh evidence of various kinds bearing on a given case, ultimately came distinctly to that conclusion. The truth was the three friends had come there with a mutual desire to see the Laird of Drammochdyle, and enjoy his 'company'. They had previously been enjoying one another's company for a good part of the day; and it was only superior diplomacy that had left Lillie in a position to pay a solemn tribute to departed worth, by enabling him to retain two threepenny bits in his pocket till the important juncture indicated, while Captain Bulkhead had gone on clearing the score as fast as it was made, with a prodigal and uncalculating readiness.

'Well, lads, we'll need to go,' said Lillie at last. 'It's a melancholy circumstance, this—vera affeckin; oh, vera. Good nicht, Ross.'

But mine host was busy supplying a lot of navvies newly off 'the pay' with liquid 'refreshment', and he heeded not the valediction.

And they went away accordingly.

Chapter XXIV

MR. CRABBICE SENIOR IS INDIGNANT

Dr. Graham's death was attributed to apoplexy, not only among the customers of the Mill Inn, but also in that veracious and trust-worthy organ of public opinion the *Strathaven Independent*, which devoted two black-bordered columns of 'leaded' type to a bio-graphical notice, commencing with the words. 'In the midst of life we are in death'; and ending in this strain, 'And so has suddenly passed away, in the rich prime of life and the full vigour of his noble intellect, one who in every relation of life was an example to the flock over whom he had been set by the great Shepherd. Hospitable in the highest degree, yet regular in his habits, faithful, zealous, earnest, indefatigable—we may not soon look upon his like again.'

The verdict of apoplexy then it were needless to dispute; only discreet parishioners thought it prudent to waive the subject as far as might be; and indiscreet ones gossiped over such stories as that to which Lillie had made reference in the Mill Inn, and other information derived through Johnnie Duncan, who, with lugu-brious countenance—partly professional perhaps, and partly the index of real sorrow at Dr. Graham's death—indulged his in-veterate love of gossip so far as to tell his 'familiars' how to a certainty the Dr. went to bed 'in a vera excitit state' at night, and was found there a 'corp' in the morning.

Of the latter fact at least there could be no doubt. And so the scene closed on Dr. Graham.

It was with somewhat of surprise, and considerably more of indignation, that Mr. Crabbice, Sen., read in next week's *Independent* an intimation requesting 'those who had claims against the late Dr. Graham to hand them in directly to Mr. Morris, of Messrs. Patten & Pendicle, who was authorised to settle the same; and to whom those indebted to the deceased would please make immediate payment.'

'Tom,' shouted the old gentleman vehemently from his own private room, and on Mr. Crabbice, Jun., answering his summons from the office, he went on, 'Did Boyce tell you of this arrangement?'.

'Which arrangement, dad?' asked Mr. Tom with the utmost affability, 'about the bond for the £500 you lent him to pay off his tradesmen; or the excambion you were kind enough to propose of twenty acres of moss and bog on your part, for an equal surface of rich arable land on his, to adjust the boundaries of your respective estates?'

'No; confound it, can't you speak common sense sometimes, sir; read that' (pointing to the notice in the *Independent*).

'Why, sir,' said Tom, 'Edward Boyce did not mention this; and probably for the best of all reasons—because he didn't know himself.'

'Didn't know—how?'

'Can't say; only he mentioned to me after the funeral that he feared he'd have a stiff job to wind up the old doctor's affairs, and he wished that somebody else had got it to do, as he feared they were in somewhat of a mess.'

'Mess; why the man died insolvent, and we're his largest creditor. Hand over the management to a mere upstart, who has no recognized position or standing! Get our claim made out in full—personal account and cash advanced on bond. I must see to the bottom of this business.'

Mr. Crabbice never, perhaps, did see to the bottom of the business so clearly as he could have wished; for, on sending in his claim, consisting of account for 'whiskies, brandies', &c., running over four or five years, along with statement of sums advanced, in security of which he had a policy of insurance on Dr. Graham's life, the whole amounting to a sum which he imagined should rather stagger the 'upstart' trustee, he had merely a note in reply, requesting him to call at the bank office and deposit the bond, and on his discharging the account, Mr. Morris's cheque would be honoured for the full amount of his claim.

The explanation was simple enough. Dr. Graham, besotted as he was, knew enough to distrust the Crabbice firm, in whose toils he lay. He had struggled, but wildly and in vain, to free himself from them, until at last, as already related, Tom Crabbice had had the audacity to deprive him, almost perforce, of a favourite pony coveted by that young gentleman, insulting him, at the same time, in the rudest and most insolent manner because he was still his debtor. Burning with shame and anger, what could the poor man do? His son-in-law, not very firm of purpose at best, was now a habitual tippler whom no man might trust; and besides, he was considerably under the power of those whose shackles himself would fain have cast off. He told his pecuniary difficulties and his grief, with tears, to his daughter, who, as has been indicated, equally with himself dreaded to make the facts known to Mr. Boyce. Mrs. Boyce was the first to suggest that they should ask counsel of Robert Morris.

Strange were the emotions in Dr. Graham's breast as the thought of the poor lame country lad who, but of yesterday as it were, came to his house day by day, a humble but earnest seeker after knowledge. He thought for a moment, and answered, 'Yes Elsie, you are right. Immutable are the eternal laws of right and wrong. The lad had faith in the right, and strove as God gave him strength to do it. I know he will not forsake a poor bewildered, misguided man, who has voluntarily surrendered the god-like within him, and yielded himself, soul and body, a slave to the meanest lusts of his nature. I can trust *him* for the aid which I should in vain look for from any of those whom—oh, bitter mockery!—I have been wont to call "my friends".'

It was arranged that Mrs. Boyce should see Robert Morris, and ask his advice. She did so, as we have already seen. Robert reckoned it a sacred duty to aid in any way he could, one to whom he owed so much. Dr. Graham, as if with a presentiment of his own early and sad death, insisted on having him legally constituted his sole executor, without loss of time. And thus it was that Mr. Crabbice, Sen., came by a bitter disappointment. Doubtless he judged rightly that Dr. Graham died insolvent; but *his* claim at least was paid in full. How they knew not, only the funds were forthcoming, and everything was settled in a business-like way, and with remarkable quietness and promptitude by the imperturbable nobody, who had deprived Mr. Crabbice, Sen., of the opportunity he had so often before enjoyed, of figuring as the trustee on a bankrupt estate, and thereby also deprived him of a lever power which he meant to work toward inclosing the laird of Drammochdyle still farther in the meshes of the net which he had begun to cast around him.

And Robert Morris was satisfied. The death of Dr. Graham had prevented his being able to relieve him from the galling yoke under which Patrick Crabbice held him; yet he had saved his name from further disgrace, and kept one thorn at least from the pillow of his only child—The means by which he did so were not, perhaps, what a 'prudent' business man would recommend, inasmuch as they involved not only *personal* risk in a pecuniary sense, but actual pecuniary sacrifice, such as it might take him years to recover.

Chapter XXV

THE MILL INN AGAIN—ITS LANDLORD UNACCOUNTABLY FINDS HIMSELF IN 'DIFFICULTIES'

IT so happened that at a certain Martinmas term Mr. George Ross, 'hotel-keeper, Mill Inn, and hotel, Strathaven', on counting over the contents of his purse carefully, found that he was short by several pounds of the sum which he was required to produce that very day to meet the rent due by him to Patrick Crabbice, Esq., the esteemed proprietor of the 'eligible and well-frequented hotel' in question. How this came about Mr. George Ross really could not tell. The like had never been before. Was it so that the various sums he had got extraneously by inheritance, through his wife, had melted away in his hands; and that his 'thriving and extensive' business had done no more for him than this? It surely could not be. Yet here was the hard fact.

Mr. George Ross knew that he had not been unduly extravagant in his expenditure; he knew that he was not an intemperate man—nobody ever saw him drunk—he only maintained himself in a reasonably 'dazed' state. In short, had merely reduced himself to that condition which seems to threaten spontaneous combustion, and sudden extinction after the manner of a 'guttered' candle end alternately—the condition which seems most homogenous with the character of a publican, pure, and simple. And if his wife did tipple a little freely now and then, as her abrupt and jerky manner at times seemed to say; and if his children were rude and ill-behaved, beyond most children, even in Strathaven, no part of all this was so very extraordinary in the circumstances. But that the Mill Inn where so much whisky was not only drunk, but duly paid for, should be a losing concern—preposterous! George, albeit he pondered over it in a bewildered kind of way as a sort of new idea which yet had come uncomfortably near home, could not see why he should be seven pounds short in his rent. But Mr. Crabbice must be faced.

'Seven pounds short, Ross! How comes that?'

'I dinna k-now, Sir. Ye see the times is bad; an' trade's been flat. So I houp ye'll hae patience for an aucht days till we see if onything comes in aboot.'

'Oh, you should look better a-head of you, Ross. That's a capital business of yours; it should be made to pay you handsomely if well managed.'

'Well, we dee oor best, Sir.'

'Couldn't you have turned you hand in some way? It disarranges my accounts not to get the money at the regular time.'

'Really, Sir, the hoose's been doin' so little this while. An' I had no live stock that I could dispose o'.'

'Well, well; I'm never disposed to be harsh with a tenant. Goodness knows I've often risked a great deal to give a man a chance of getting on. But I've observed that the place has been going out of repair for some time. Now, you know, Ross, that will never do about an hotel.'

'Aye, but ance the term was past I'm gettin' up the painters to renew the letterin' on the sign-boord, an' put in some new panes o' gless.'

'New panes of glass? D'ye mean to say they're are actually broken windows allowed in the house a single day?'

'Oh, it was only an oonexpeckit accident the ither nicht, an' I haena been doon the toon sin syne to tell the painter about it.'

'An accident—how?'

'Oh, weel ye ken Maister Crabbice fowk will fyles hae a bit frolic.'

'Frolic! I should think breaking windows no great frolic. I hope you don't let the character of your house be damaged by drunken brawls taking place in it?

'Oh, fye na—naething o' the sort I assure ye. It was only twa chaps 't got some noisy; but they war oot o' the hoose by that time. They war a' i' the furth afore the tane brak the window wi's steekit neive.'

'Well—that was not very seemly. However, I've no time to discuss the thing to-day—I'll send Mr. Tom round some day soon to take a look of your stock. See and get that balance of seven pounds by this day week—Goodday.'

And Tom, who some six months before had abruptly broken off his visits at the Mill Inn, which, however, was still the haunt of Lillie and others, his companions, including Edward Boyce, was sent accordingly. How unceremoniously he treated poor George Ross; how he pried into his matters, domestic, and financial, how even he criticised the battered state of his pewter whisky measures need not be stated. Perhaps the climax was reached when he came to the 'posting dipartment', and found it now reduced to the old delapidated hostler, Davie Beaton, a red spavined horse, and a gaunt-looking dog cart. At this point Tom uttered a volley of oaths.

'Hang it, Ross, this is shameful not to have a decent looking horse about the place.'

'Ye ken, Mr. Tom, there's vera little eese for them noo—the road's fairly deen for sin' railways cam' into the countra.'

'Pshaw you blockhead. There's the man over the way has a pair of good roadsters out every day in single or double harness.'

'But he has a great run o' commercial fowk, ye see.'

'And why shouldn't you have the same.'

'Ye canna tak awa yer neebours custom.'

'Nor yet keep your own it would seem—such a place, everything in disorder or broken to the very door-bell and wheelbarrow. 'Pon my word the governor'll go frantic if he sees this.'

Enough to say that on Tom's report being given in, Mr. Crabbice, Sen., decided forthwith that George Ross could be tenant of the Mill Inn no longer than the expiry of the current year.

Chapter XXVI

THE LICENSING COURT OF THE BURGH OF STRATHAVEN— AN APPEAL TAKEN

It was the April licensing court, and the four Baillies of Strathaven took their seats on the Bench, to say how many 'inhabiters' there should be allowed to hold licences to sell strong waters for behoof of their fellow town's folks. The population of the place, speaking roundly, was barely 10,000, and the number of places actually licensed, in one shape or another, to sell 'beer and spirits, porter and ales', was the modest figure of sixty-five; or something like one to every 150 men, women, and children. The number of applicants for licence on the occasion under notice, was 70; being an increase of five.

Mr. Crabbice, Sen., who had an eye to the Provostship of Strathaven had kindly consented to accept office as a Baillie at the preceding election, as a step toward the higher office. He now presided in absence of the Provost, who had become effete for some time past through old age and general stupidity, and what he and his three borther magistrates, the other Baillies—plain traders and shop-keepers of the place, whose names need not be immortalised in these pages—had to consider, was whether all these, or how many, should be granted licence certificates.

Now, it so happened that the Temperance Society of Strathaven, of which Robert Morris, as a staunch advocate of total abstinence, had been made 'President', (every concern must have its president, you see), had taken this question of the proportion of licensed houses to population into serious consideration, and, on the court-day craved to be heard by their honours, the Baillies, on the subject. The Temperance Society was an institution Mr. Crabbice held in supreme contempt; and when Robert Morris, accompanied by some of its leading members, appeared in presence of the Bench to present its memorial and state their case, he scarcely made an effort to conceal that contempt.

On the opposite side appeared Mr. Daniel Lillie, 'solicitor' with what he was pleased to call 'the petition of the inhabitants', in favour specially of the new applicants for licence.

After the memorial, which prayed for a reduction—not an increase—of the number of licenses, had been read, Robert Morris followed it up by a few plain sentences, showing, from hard statistics, that seven-eighths of the crime and pauperism of the country are attributable to the use of intoxicating drinks—the police and poor-law reports of Strathaven itself being evidence—and that there was no doubt drunkenness increased in proportion to the facilities for, and temptations to, indulgence in strong drink.

Mr. Lillie, who to all appearance had worshipped devoutly at the shrine of Bacchus, that very morning replied that 'this was a free country'. 'No more sacred right has descended to us, your honours, than that glorious liberty of the subject won by our noble forefathers. Let every man', continued Mr. L., 'be equally free and independent—beware how you curtail our heaven-sent privileges.' From this flight he descended to take up the cases for which he had been specially retained, and to point out the peculiar hardships that would be inflicted upon some of the applicants by refusal. 'There, for example, your honours, is the case of the applicant, George Ross, who asks a licence for a spirit-shop, in that house, No. 30, Batter Lane. A licenced house is wanted in the locality; there is none between it and the top of the Lane—no less than thirty doors off—counting both sides of the Lane. The applicant, a man of irreproachable character, has given up his present place of business—the Mill Inn—his respectable management of which can be spoken to by, at least, one of your honours; he has leased these premises which are well adapted to the purpose; and if your honours should refuse the licence his loss will be very severe—nay ruinous. But you cannot—I know will not prostitute the high powers with which you have been entrusted by your Sovereign in this way.'

Their honours looked wise, as was proper in the circumstances, and one of them observed that Batter Lane was 'a bad locality for a public. There's no commerce there. It's inhabited only by workin' folk.'

'Your honour,' replied Mr. Lillie, 'I go upon the great general principle, that all men in this free land have equal rights and privileges. You cannot—you dare not, say that the working man has not a perfect title to have due facility for supplying his wants as well as the highest in the land.'

'Weel, but, Deniel,' said the plain spoken magistrate, 'we canna alloo an incress o' public hooses i' the toon, that's clear aneuch.'

'I appeal to the great principles of law and justice—I—I appeal to Mr. Crabbice at yer right hand, there. He knows—hic—Mr. Ross; yes; aye, and he'll see him put right—'

A severe frown from Patrick Crabbice, Esq., had failed to check Lillie's talk, and Mr. C. fearing indiscreet unttterances from the eloquent lawyer, broke in emphatically—'The Bench will now give their opinions. Silence.'

The opinions of the other two Baillies coincided entirely with that of him who had uttered himself. So they agreed—the Preses rather sulkily dissenting—that in face of the facts 'so ably brought before them, it was the duty of the Magistrates of this town not to increase the number of licence certificates, but rather to seize every available opportunity of reducing them.'

And on going over the list in detail, they found 'that no additional spirit shop was required in any quarter' of Strathaven.

'On behalf of my client, Mr. George Ross, I beg to appeal to the court of Quarter Sessions,' said Mr. Lillie.

The Court, thereafter, broke up. And Mr. Crabbice, with a very explosive countenance, rose, and stiffly left the Bench, without the courtesy of even bidding his brother Baillies goodbye. These worthy magistrates, however, took the matter more coolly. They remained behind the upbreak of the court, for a 'sociable crack', and one of their number, Baillie Fobister, a pudgy, and on the whole comfortable-looking man, with no particular expression in his face, whose head was peculiar in so far as it narrowed away upward and all round from his puffy-looking cheeks to the top, who was a fishcurer by profession, but when he stood up in speechmaking, himself always reminded one of an overgrown seal that had learnt to talk, and now rose on its dorsal fin to give you a discourse—he took out his silver snuff-box, which had been presented to him on some memorable occasion, and gave his 'colleagues' a pinch. He was a really benevolent, single-minded man—in so far as mind existed within him—and his instincts were in the main right. So although he had not spoken before audibly, he now expressed emphatically his belief that the Bench had been 'rightly guided' in this weighty business. 'Nae doot, gentlemen, its a ooncommon orranous thing to decide against the interests o' a man like Mr. Crabbice—it is. But we've public duties to perform, gentlemen, we're public men—joodges o' the kwintra, in fack—an' we maun dee fat's richt, be the consequence 'at may.'

'Aye, aye,' responded another of the Bench, 'as the Roman poet says—*fiat justiciar*—I foryet the exack words, but it means that we're to dee justice though the lift sud fa' an' smore the laverocks. Crabbice 'll appeal, nae doot, an' I sanna mervel though he carry't there. He has enfluence amo' the Justices, ye see; aye has he.

'Aweel, aweel,' replied Baillie Fobister, 'we maun gie oor decision accordin' to oor conscience. It's quite irrevelant to the Bench fat he may dee in anither judicatur.'

Thereafter the Bench adjourned.

Chapter XXVII

THE MANSION-HOUSE OF VATVILLE— THE PROSPECTS OF SOME OF THE CRABBICE FAMILY, AND THE PURPOSES OF MR. CRABBICE, SENIOR

'Run, Eliza, and see that the covers are laid—papa's home in bad humour with something or other; and if the dinner's kept waiting he'll be perfect verocious.'

'But, mamma, Captain Ryrie's not come.'

' 'Pon my word no! And he a'most one of ourselves now too. Well how lucky the Captain's to be here; he's such a jewel of a man, and always keeps papa in such good humour.'

'Yes, mamma, *his* temper I know is *so* good.

'Aye what a treasure he'll be, dear Eliza, when you go to the Grove his happy bride.'

So Mrs. Crabbice's match-making had come to something at last. And not a bad result after all, for Eliza was pleased, Mrs. Crabbice herself was delighted even to extacy, insomuch that she could hardly refrain from hugging the gallant Captain about the neck, and kissing his purple countenance; and Patrick Crabbice doted on the notion of the great wealth possessed by his prospective son-in-law.

Mr. Crabbice, sen., did come home in bad temper on the day of the licensing court, and he spoke but little, notwithstanding the mollifying presence of Captain Ryrie, until dinner was nearly finished. He then broke out in proper style to the Captain, Tom being also an auditor, upon the pitiful, contracted notions of those petty traders, his brother magistrates in Strathaven, who could be swayed by a parcel of ignorant fanatics, and refuse to industrious well doing men the means of making an honest livelihood.

'Confounded shabby, say I,' echoed Captain Ryrie in a spasmodic way, as he was still eating, and the Captain could not well do two things at once, least of all when taking his dinner was one of the two.

'But I say Tom,' asked Mr. Crabbice, 'what the deuce made that fool, Lillie, bring Ross's case so prominently up—and blether out our connection with him.'

'Can't say,' answered Tom.

'You were surely not mad enough to instruct him to do it?'

'I should think not, dad. But his own amiable feelings carried him off, I daresay. He and Ross are great cronies.'

'He's losing *caste* that man, as a lawyer—I must consider what's to be done with him. You see,' explained Mr. Crabbice, turning to the Captain, 'Ross has been doing no good in the Mill Inn. So we've resolved to displenish him at the ensuing term—in fact the Inn is let already to another, a very substantial man, who was in want of a good opening. Ross made a great ado about it, of course; but I had the thing entirely in my own hand, he wasn't able to square accounts with me, and I could and would have poinded him, if he hadn't given up the lease.'

'Aye, aye—quite right,' said the captain.

'However, he has now come to see that it is the best thing for him. There will just be about enough to meet all claims when his effects are sold off, and leave him his necessary bits of house furniture—a cartload or so. But you know, Captain, I would never treat a man harshly; so as the ground floor of that piece of property of mine in Batter Lane has been without a tenant for a couple of years, I've let it to Ross; and have no doubt he could do a very good business in it among the working classes. It is centrical you see for a whole lot of them the worse paid kind of labouring and handicraft people—who, let me tell you, are good consumers. Why, we supply five to eight pounds' value of raw whisky per week to some similar houses; and I mean, even yet, to give Ross some stock on credit for a short term. But here these upstart fellows come forward, and at the cry of a set of teetotallers, refuse a licence. It's really too bad.'

'Confounded shabby,' said the captain.

'Appeal the case,' said Tom.

'Appeal! Certainly I will—that is, I'll get it appealed.'

'Ap-pealed?' said Captain Ryrie, not very certain apparantly what that signified.

'Yes, to the Quarter Sessions you know, Captain—all of us county gentlemen have seats there you know.'

'Oh bless me, yes. Aye, aye, so we have,' said the Captain in great delight, 'and these poor beggars, who are only burgh baillies, have not—have they?'

'No Captain, not one of them has the qualification to get on the Commission of the Peace,' said Mr. C., stretching himself up in full dignity.

'First rate!' exclaimed Captain Ryrie.

'Here,' said Mr. Crabbice, waxing didactic, 'is the great advantage of our mixed Constitution. Our legislation proceeds in all cases from the lower to the higher tribunal. Here at least before the Quarter Sessions the case will have an impartial hearing. Here is the value of having judicial powers, in the last resort, in the hands of those who are above the influence of petty local prejudices and crotchets, not to say sordid considerations.'

Captain Ryrie was so lost in amazement at this burst of eloquence, that he could only stare and grunt. He swallowed a full glass of port and stared more.

'The Sessions sit next week,' said Tom.

'Yes,' replied Mr. Crabbice, 'and we must not lose a day in making preparation. Let's see how the Bench can be arranged. There's Sir Joshua—who is sure to be there as preses—a high-minded man, but full of whims sometimes—his vote can't be safely counted upon, though he generally goes against the burgh magistrates. Then there's Heddles of Weetmire—we can reckon upon him; there's Macveerie of Rappoch, he can be managed by a little tackling beforehand, if Sir Joshua don't speak on the wrong side during the sitting; and Topwell of Bibster—we've a large account against him. Then there's yourself, Captain, and poor Boyce—Tom will bring him up—five votes, and my own, in case it should be absolutely required. We'll, that would turn't, I'm convinced. But I'd rather not vote myself. Do you think of any one else, Captain?'

'Eh! surely—there's Willy Grant of Glentrockit, was at the Grove the other nicht.'

'Willy Grant!' exclaimed Tom with a loud laugh, 'He never sat on the Strathaven Bench in his life I'm sure; he *would* look rather primitive down from his native hills in his hodden grey.'

'What of that,' aswered Mr. Crabbice, senior, severely. 'Mr. Grant holds the sacred trust of Her Majesty's Commission of the Peace; and his vote is as good as that of any titled nobleman.'

And so it proved.

On the day before the meeting of Quarter Sessions, Willy Grant, a pastoral sort of character, who held a miniature and rather barren estate in the upland part of the county, Edward Boyce, whose invitations to Vatville had of late been few and far between, and sundry other Justices of the Peace were all Mr. Crabbice's guests at a jolly dinner at Vatville. To-morrow's business was talked over, and a revised forecast of the voting taken. Willy Grant, whose trafficking lay mainly amongst sheep and goats, and who, true to native traditions, was conversant with nothing else save sneeshin and whisky, was of course quite new to the whole business, and he required to be instructed as to the importance of his vote and the mode of exercising it. If a rather obtuse pupil, he was at least a willing one; and the lesson he had to learn was one he could scarcely misunderstand or forget: it being simply this, that when the clerk called the names for a division, 'Refuse' or 'Grant' the licence certificate, he was, like a true Highlandman, to be faithful to his clan, and merely utter his own patronymic,——Grant.

On the day of the Quarter Sessions, 'a full bench of Justices met', there being, as the local organ of public opinion averred, 'a great amount of important business to transact'. Sir Joshua Krustie occupied his usual position of president, and expounded law points with his usual air of authority, freely quoting those scraps of dog latin which lawyers occasionally use, and which he, not being a lawyer, liked all the better to repeat. It were utterly needless to recapitulate the arguments used by the burgh fiscal in support of the judgment of the Strathaven Baillies, refusing license certificates to 'George Ross, 30, Batter Lane', and four others, seeing the law was laid down from the Bench, that the local judges had no right to deal differently with different applicants—to grant licenses to sixty-five and refuse to other five. To Mr. Crabbice's infinite delight, the President declared that this would be 'applying the *lextalionis* to those whose applications were refused' which was intolerable! So in the case of George Ross and his brother appellants, the vote stood seven to four in favour of a reversal of the decision of the local Magistrates—'Mr. Crabbice of Vatville declining to vote.'

Directly on this decision being given, Mr. Crabbice, senior, and two or three more, his friends, left the Court. They had discharged their public duty for the time, and now went to look after their private interests. Their departure was noticeable, inasmuch as the great part of the business for which the Quarter Sessions had assembled was yet to be done; and inasmuch as, when two or three other exactly similar appeals from country districts came up they were promptly dismissed, because Sir Joshua and others held that the multiplication of public houses in rural districts was a great evil, which ought to be discouraged by all available means; and that therefore the local Justices, who were best able to judge of the circumstances, had acted with great propriety in refusing licenses.

Perhaps the persons interested in those cases were not aware of the mode in which that noble institution the Quarter Sessions may be worked for the public behoof; perhaps *they* had not influence to enable them to 'arrange' a bench beforehand.

Chapter XXVIII

FACILIS DESCENSUS

The history of Edward Boyce for the two or three years that succeeded the death of his father-in-law, is quickly told. If that event temporarily roused him to reflection, and some feeble resolutions of amendment, the baneful influence of Tom Crabbice, backed by the craving for stimulants, which in place of having sufficient determination to crush and conquer, he had fostered and fed, soon led him into the downward path again. Late nights out continued, and scenes of domestic discomfort—(for the very sight of his dispirited heart-sore wife, pained or irritated him according to the state of drunkenness, or after-drunkenness, he might be in at the time)—alternated with fitful intervals of revived affection and unduly demonstrative kindness.

Latterly, however, the younger Crabbice had sought his company but seldom. It was believed he had led Edward Boyce into undertaking pecuniary responsibilities for him in certain questionable transactions of his, which dared not meet the paternal eye, and that Edward had got the amount to pay for his friend. A quarrel had ensued, but after mutual recriminations, Mr. Boyce had seen the propriety of keeping quiet on this particular subject, as Tom had not failed to warn him that he had very precise information about scenes in which Edward Boyce had been an actor, that it might not be to his comfort nor credit to have revealed.

The then eldest child of Mr. and Mrs. Boyce, grown to be an engaging girl of five years of age, took ill of measles and died. Her father had been as deeply attached to her as it was possible for one in his state to be; but in place of her death affecting him with a manly sorrow, after a passionate outburst of grief he rushed into excess more wildly than ever.

He might now be seen in the streets of Strathaven at mid-day, visibly tipsy, unshaven, dirty, careless of even the appearance of respectability in dress, and—it need hardly be said—coolly 'cut' by Tom Crabbice.

'Have I no friends, then?' the poor misguided fellow bitterly asked himself, on meeting Tom and some friends of his without any other than left-headed recognition from them. Something within even yet faintly whispered Yes—'The younger Crabbice may pass you with a sneer when it suits him, and the older Crabbice may regard you only with that peculiar interest which the vulture has in the writhing victim that will by and bye gorge his maw; but the world yet contains those who would really act a friend's part.'

'Would God I could take Morris's advice, and give up that cursed drink,' he muttered as he staggered along. 'I need some one to guide me.'

'Some one to guide him was not long wanting; for before he had gained the end of the street he encountered Lillie in a state of extreme exasperation at the Crabbices, senior and junior. Ever since his unlucky appearance before the licensing magistrates, the elder Crabbice had treated Lillie very curtly, in addition to giving him a special 'blowing up'.

'But what d'ye think—the old villain told me to-day—that I'm to have no more of his court or factorship business, and he has actually handed over the drawing out o' his daughter's marriage contract to that sneak Sharkey.'

Edward Boyce stared stupidly as he repeated 'Marriage contract!—What contract?'

'Oh, you know Crabbice's eldest daughter 's to be married to Ryrie o' the Grove. All settled at last. 'Pon my word a bonny match 'twill be.'

'Eliza Crabbice is to be married to Captain Ryrie?'

'Yes: your pardon, Mr. Boyce—the pert doll-faced beauty that the old madam wished to hook your own self with. But she was out there at any rate, and served her right—No Crabbice that ever breathed was worthy of being a wife to Edward Boyce my truest friend on earth.'

Whether Edward Boyce exactly relished Lillie's fervour it

would be difficult to say. He stood with a considerably embarrassed and very stupid look, as if such reflections as he had were not of the most comfortable sort possible, while the lawyer pulled off his beaver by its very flabby brim, looked inside it among some greasy papers, and after dexterously clapping it on his head again without spilling them, re-commenced his tirade against Mr. Crabbice, 'Reproach *me* with my drunken habits, the villain; and yet take this man, this gross unmitigated brute, as his son-in-law. Why, Ryrie, the dull, phlegmatic beast, 'll drink as much port in a week as would drown us both, Mr. Boyce. But, of course, *he* is never *seen* tipsy—tumbles into bed nightly like a big swine, as he is, and by next morning is as sober—no, as drearily dull and stagnant as ever. And to be reproach't by Crabbice, o' all men—Confound it, but I'll expose him, and his tricks and rascalities, 'fore Heaven and earth, I will.'

This was mere vapour, however, as Lillie pretty well knew; for it has to be observed in the first place, that Lillie could not now afford to part with Mr. Crabbice, so long as there was hope of getting work of any sort from him; and Crabbice had taken care to leave margin for some vague hope of that sort; then in the second place, while an exposure from Lillie might, and would, have been dreaded by Crabbice at one time, he had now reduced himself to a position in which a threat of that sort, coming from him, could be treated with contempt; because, as Crabbice knew very well, the world would give but little heed to the babbling of a broken-down drunken lawyer.

'And he deserves it too,' answered Edward—'show them up, Lillie, both father and son.'

'I'm hanged if I don't; for that scoundrel Tom gave me the most outrageous insolence simply for refusing to do dirty work for him out o' the old man's sight.'

'Just like him, too—but he'll land himself in a scrape too some o' these days.'

'If he don't, no thanks to his own virtues, or to my most sincere prayers,' said Lillie, who had a kind of notion that Tom possessed a rather remarkable faculty in getting out of scrapes and leaving others in. 'But that won't mend matters greatly with me, Mr. Boyce. After selling myself, soul and body, to do that man's work for all these years; after he had made other people distrust me, to have his own business taken away next, as if I had ever spared

my best efforts to gain his ends, or ever embezzled a shilling o'
his cash. 'Pon my word, Mr. Boyce, this is a hard world. If it
were not for one or two generous hearted fellows like yourself,
I don't know what it would come to.'

The truth is, Lillie was excessively dry, as well as indignant;
and the result was that, with little persuasion, he managed to lead
Edward Boyce to 30, Batter Lane, where they found their old
friend, George Ross, ready to receive and welcome them.

The place was one of those dreary dens, that are, unhappily,
too common to need description. It contained, besides a sort of
kitchen, a couple of rooms, pretty much of a piece in appearance;
and each furnished with a table, some rickety chairs, a long deal
form, and a spittoon or two, and stinking of whisky and tobacco
smoke. The master and mistress, both still in what should have
been the early prime of life, bore each pretty distinct tokens of
the particular line of business to which they had devoted themselves, in their bleared, unblessed countenances. The children,
poor things, were dirty, pert, and unmannerly to a degree, even
as compared with the state of things at the Mill Inn.

Lillie called for drink, and it was supplied, George himself
officiating as waiter, pewter gill stoup in hand; and in one of those
dingy back rooms, with several chance companions, not of the
choicest character, the two spent some hours, amid a good deal
of insane noise and mirth. Mine host, who, as an old friend, was
particularly glad to see the laird in his new establishment, did his
best to keep up the general hilarity; which George was the better
able to do, as he was just then of opinion that the Batter Lane
house was to 'do pretty weel', he being now free of the burden
of the 'posting department' and other adjuncts, which, by his
experience, did not pay. In now relying mainly on the 'hard stuff'
for his profits, he was sanguine of better results.

And that night after he gone home, perfectly maddened with
whisky of the vilest description, Edward Boyce signalised the
precise depth to which he had fallen, by actually striking the wife
of his bosom with his fists—seizing her by the hair, and dashing
her to the floor, in the very same fashion as any one of those rude
and vulgar blackguards with whom he had associated that evening might have done; and all because, even yet, she had sat up
to wait his coming, and minister to his comfort, so far as that
might be possible.

Chapter XXIX

CAPTAIN RYRIE'S WEDDING

It was not in the nature of things that a man of such local position as the proprietor of the Grove should get married without the subject being much and variously discussed. That were indeed an insignificant wedding, which in respect of the covert brutality, the unprincipled heartlessness, the spurious pretensions, the awkward boobyism, the blinded—misguided affection—of the bridegroom—poor man; and the pert 'forwardness', the trumpery beauty, the undeniable grimness, the finical nicety and desperate extravagance, the slatternly habits, and shrewish temper of the bride, did not furnish topics of engrossing talk to their acquaintances generally. The truth, my worthy Sir, is that we each and all of us love a quiet morsel of gossip. And if my stedfast friend find occasion to make me the subject of gratifying that love, shall I thenceforth forswear his, or her company for ever? Nay verily; let me take the thing more philosophically; for why should my ridiculous peculiarities escape the comment they very likely merit. I shall only hope that my friend will never descend to what is ill natured or unjust toward me, nor hear others do so without a protest in my behalf; and with a very firm promise that my conduct shall at least never traverse that rule toward him or her we may shake hands and jog on as cordially as of old.

A marriage then invites the legitimate exercise of the gossiping faculty. The man and woman stand forth in face of the world all in all to each other, apart from the world's opinion; and Heaven help them if idle or caustic words can mar the serenity of their thoughts.

Not that it could have been quite grateful to Captain Ryrie or Miss Crabbice to have heard every sentiment that was uttered by the community of Strathaven in relation to their wedding. For in the Kirktown, whither Johnnie Duncan—now fulfilling the office of the beadle under another parson than Dr. Graham, and whom for long Johnnie rather patronised as a 'raw lad', who needed some direction from one of his ripe experience in the sacred office—had first carried the tidings—in the Kirktown there were very candid and homely sayings spoken of the marriage. As, for example, when Mrs. Muggart had told the news to her friend Mrs. Ellison, and the latter matron, with commendable tact for once, simply replied.

'Tut, ye're jokin me noo, Mrs. Muggart.'

'Tell ye me an' I be jokin' a forteen-days aifter this than.'

'Oh, an' it's to be immedantly than?' answered Mrs. Ellison, who had really wished to get at that point, she having, unknown to Mrs. Muggart, heard a 'sloom' of the coming event before. 'Na, Sirs; but he's a gruesome, ill faur't carl; that leddy creaters is nae ill to please, weel-a-wat.'

'Deed no; only it's jist the thing 't they're brocht up till 'oman by their nain pawrents—marry ony aul' debush't slype, providin' he can gie them a richt doon-sit.'

'Eh aye, Eppie, its owre true. I'm seer nedder you nor me, fan we wus young lasses, wud hae ta'en that blotch't, drucken, ugsome breet for gowd nor siller,' said Mrs. Ellison, sticking her hands in her sides, and glancing across with justifiable pride to the souter, who sat busily reading his paper with grimy face, a rough beard of nearly a week's growth on his chin, his unkempt hair straggling about the margins of his countenance, and a snuffy drop at the tip of his big resonant nose.

In only another case shall we listen to a fragment of the current gossip: and this in the home of our acquaintance, Robert Morris. James Munro, with his wonted decision, had pronounced the marriage a perfectly commendable and proper one.

'Aye, Jamie, an' that's what your notions of marriage are comin' to?' said Robert, laughing.

'My notions o' marriage, Robbie, are precisely what they always have been,' was the reply.

'Well, I daresay there 'll be no great waste o' spurious sentimentality in the matter, at least. The captain's no a man likely to indulge in extremly hyperbolical language, even in love.'

'No; an' *that*, let me tell you, is something freen'. But more than that; baith bride and bridegroom are probably as deeply stirred in their affection toward each other as it's possible for them to be. You can readily fancy, now, that Eliza Crabbice's rosy cheeks, smirking countenance, an' daintily-dressed person, present to Captain Ryrie as attractive a picture of female loveliness as that operose warrior's mind and heart could conceive of, or understand—Can you not?'

'No doubt of it.'

'He, at least, is not the man to whom you would put the question Kingsley puts somewhere—''Was it a face you worshipped, or the soul that shone through the face?'' What, to him, were the gleam of earnest, glowing intelligence, from the depths of eyes whose glance can reach your inmost heart, as it lights into glorious radiance features that *may* be plain, for aught you can tell, but which, so long as you hold the immortal mind and spirit superior to the material prison in which they are confined, you find it impossible to make out to be so; or, indeed, to criticise at all in respect of the detail o' their mere external contour.'

Robert Morris who, as was wont, had been in the vein to treat his friend's theorisings with a free and easy jocularity, as if struck by some sudden thought, assumed a slightly grave and constrained aspect during the utterance of these words. Was it possible that that flight could call up a distinctly outlined vision of some absent form before his mind's eye? Who can tell. At its close he remained silent and abstracted, till his sister, who was sewing at the opposite window, toward which she looked, turned to James with the sly remark—'I understood that you considered common sense, and not hyperbole, a desirable quality in the language used in such matters!'

'Be it so, Lizzie; but if ye speak from real feeling—not from shallow sentimentalism, which has never really moved your heart at all—ye winna do violence to common sense, though your words may seem passionate enough.'

'Well you have finished the sketch o' the Captain an' the bride he *might* get—but what about the one he is to get?'

'Yes, Jamie,' Robert broke in—'Ye had to make out that the marriage was a perfectly commendable and proper one.'

'An' it's easily done. If Captain Ryrie is incapable of appreciatin' or understandin' a nobler style of woman, Miss Crabbice, for aught I know, is equally incapable of understandin' or appreciatin' a better style of man. She would measure any man as a husband solely by his position an' his cash. Thus each finds in the ither elements for the exercise of the highest regard of which their affections severally are capable, and, therefore, their marriage is commendable and proper.'

'So, if men generally were dull enough to see only the beauty, that is but skin deep, and women avaricious enough to make money their chief object o' desire, we should soon have none but model marriages?'

'No Lizzie: I don't speak such nonsense. Captain Ryrie's marriage is no more a model marriage than he is a model man; but if he chooses a wife whose moral level is the same as his own, and on account of qualities for which I should heartily despise her, there is a fitness in the thing which no one can dispute. And they should find (and probably will find) in their marriage all they expected of it. But that, let me say, is very different from what I should expect, or could bear to think of finding in it.'

We are not prepared to say how far Mrs. Crabbice's practical views in matrimony would have coincided with those of the combative young man who has been declaring himself thus. But there is probable ground for the belief that Captain Ryrie, until he was taken in hand by Mrs. Crabbice, had really no idea what a frisky young man he was. True, it was now well on to thirty years since he resigned the commission he had the honour to hold from His Majesty in the militia of his native county, so that he could not be altogether so juvenile as a young lady very dear to him who was not then born. Yet when nudged on the elbow by this familiar matron, when pulled up to the serious exertion of dancing at her evening parties, when joked by her on his flirtations which she knew about—ah, didn't she?—it was not easy for the Captain to resist the notion that there must after all, be a fund of gallantry within him which somehow had hitherto lain latent, and unknown to him.

And thus was the gallant if unwarlike soldier led—(no, not like an ox to the shambles, because Eliza Crabbice was, as everybody should know, a nice young lady, and the Captain emphatically declared that he had been in love with her to a serious degree for ever so long)—but thus, let us say, was he led on to the hymeneal altar. We do not mean to aver that he ever made any such fervid declarations of love to Eliza herself, for he was not a demonstrative man; only he did so to her mother, when the old lady had fairly driven him into a corner, and he stated it in a general way to various other people.

This matrimonial alliance between the houses of Crabbice and Ryrie was, as has been already indicated, regarded with a large measure of satisfaction by the greater portion of the Crabbice family. Mrs. Crabbice was, of course, delighted in a special degree, for was not the match one of her own making. Patrick Crabbice, Esq., was pleased in a less demonstrative, but very solid kind of way; for his satisfaction was based mainly on an 'instrument', legally executed, which provided that, in the event of Capt. Ryrie's decease taking place, the Grove, with all its 'pertinents and adjuncts'—'failing male heirs, should pass to the said Eliza Crabbice or Ryrie, lawful spouse of the aforesaid Benjamin Ryrie.' As for Tom Crabbice, he had at first uttered certain oaths, at the idea of his sister marrying a dotard hunks that might be her grandfather. But since it had to be, Tom was not the man to raise any serious protest against it. She might marry the King of the Cannibal Islands for him. And Miss Maria Crabbice wound up certain criticisms of the bridegroom's person by declaring, in her own amiable way, that 'the old militia-man might get a worse nurse for his declining days than Eliza.'

The marriage day, it need hardly be said, was a great day, though on this head we must be content to say *vide Strathaven Independent* of that date, and pass on toward the wind-up of this history.

Chapter XXX

ROBERT MORRIS ON BUSINESS IN ENGLAND

It is a striking thing to observe how, even in the most stagnant circles of humanity, a series of important changes affecting the condition of life, or the tenure of life itself, will now and again occur within a brief period. After years of quiescence, and every body going on as usual, there come changes in quick succession, by incidents of good or bad fortune, by marriages or deaths, till the constitution of *our* society is essentially changed, and those of us who are most engrossed with this earth's toils and pleasures perforce must feel, however transiently, that 'Here we have no continuing city'. To even the humblest and most obscure the thought will occasionally come home, in some vague shape, if thought ever comes at all, that

> Our little systems have their day,
> They have their day, and cease to be.

And so, in the community of Strathaven, as we shall see.

Robert Morris had been absent on a journey, on business in the north of England—the first he had undertaken of the kind, but Mr. Patten had to confess that he too was now 'failed', and unequal to such fatigue. Curiously it happened that, though Robert's business did not take him off the Great East Coast route, save at the point where he diverged to reach a large manu-facturing town, he found himself one day, after he had started for homeward, 'breaking his journey' at an intermediate station, and, after a pretty long drive per special postboy, putting up at a wayside inn, and anon wending his way to a comfortable looking country mansion, to which he certainly had no invitation whatever, mentally apostrophising the scenery around in a mechanical sort of way, in lines such as these—

> The stately homes of England,
>   How beautiful they stand
> Amid their tall ancestral trees,
>   O'er all the pleasant land.

The truth was, Robert had a friend there, whom he felt he must call upon, and while he knew that the visit was unexpected, and might be inopportune—requiring apology in fact—he had an instinctive confidence that any lack of etiquette, or other infelicity in the matter, would be blundered over somehow, and that he would be received with at least sincere and honest, and not simulated feeling.

The friend in question was of course Agnes Wilson, who was governess in the family whose mansion Robert intruded himself upon. We don't mean, however, to give any particular account here of the interview that occurred. Only, lest the reader should fancy that it was a piece of courtship, he had better disabuse his mind of that. They talked, as sensible people would, of Strathaven and its belongings; of the remanent members of the Morris family, and of James Munro.

'I thought that friend of yours very clever,' said Agnes.

'And so he is,' answered Robert, with the honest feeling that James was really clever as compared with himself.

'And he is such a frank and manly-looking fellow.'

'Yes, his manner, and physical appearance as well, commend him to you also,' said Robert, again quite conscious of his own inferiority—keenly conscious of how little *he* had to recommend him in that way.

Agnes next asked about George Ross, and learnt with surprise of what she called his 'deplorable' position at 30, Batter Lane.

Then they talked of Drammochdyle and the household there, so sadly changed; how Edward Boyce had become lost even to the sense of ordinary propriety in his conduct; how, while his wife pleaded with Agnes, as her most intimate friend, to come and stay with her whenever she could, Agnes felt the utmost difficulty about the matter, as believing that the Edward Boyce that now was, would really not give her cordial welcome. And yet, when she thought of sweet Elsie Graham, the companion of her childhood and girlhood, dejected, nearly heart-broken, ill used, in failing health, and with no friend to confide her griefs to, what would she not have given to be near her.

Then for a moment they diverged to the grand marriage at the Grove, of which Agnes had heard. 'And so the Crabbice family will, by and bye, be prominently established among your "landed gentry", as the head of that house would say,' said Agnes, playfully.

'No doubt,' was Robert's reply, 'but as for the head of the house and founder of the "family" himself, I have heard, only yesterday, that he is gone to a region where, probably, such distinctions cannot be much valued by those who grasp them most fondly here.'

It appeared, indeed, that Patrick Crabbice, Esq., in the midst of his important and engrossing labours, had been brought suddenly up by what Johnnie Duncan termed 'a stroke o' blastin',' and after lingering a few days had died. And a copy of the *Strathaven Independent* had reached our friend, in the printing of which the publisher had had to turn up three of his 'column rules' to form a black border, for a 'double-leaded' biographical notice, headed 'The late Patrick Crabbice, Esq.'

So it was; 'the solemn event' had come 'unexpectedly, almost suddenly', and after 'a few days of severe sufferings'—(we omit the latter part of the sentence about the kind of 'fortitude' with which the sufferings were borne, because it was literally untrue)—Patrick Crabbice was no more. 'Cut down in the midst of'—his grasping, worldly schemes, shall we also substitute for the more flattering editorial estimate of his pursuits. Probably we may, and yet be at least equally true to the man's life and death.

Chapter XXXI

THE WILD OATS ARE SOWN—IS THE CROP FULL-EARED GOLDEN GRAIN?

By about the time of his father's death, Tom Crabbice had pretty well sown his crop of wild oats. So at least it would appear. He was now fully thirty, and had led on the whole a distinctly vicious life. For a good many years, he had been wont to get drunk not unfrequently, and to do very disgraceful deeds while in that state; for Tom's powers of deliberate mischief failed him not, even when tipsy. It was sufficiently well known that he had habitually associated with very questionable companions, both male and female. Yet here he was, settling down a man reputedly of steady business habits, and, despite the sceptical notions of a few inconsiderable people, who could not believe that in the moral world, any more than in the physical world, purity is attained by wallowing in a dunghill, he came, in a marvellously short space of time, to be recognised as a man of established 'character'. At the annual meeting of the Strathaven Society for the promotion of general philanthropy, he had, by request, moved a resolution declaring the necessity of special efforts to improve the moral condition of 'the lapsed masses'; and in doing so he was introduced to the meeting by the chairman—none other than Sir Joshua Krustie—as 'the worthy son of a worthy father, and who promises most creditably to fill the sad blank in the management of our benevolent institutions, caused by the demise of my most excellent friend'. Tom was gaining status in every respect; for being of the Presbyterian persuasion, what could the Parson do

126

next but agitate for his election as a 'ruling elder', which was duly accomplished.

A contrast rather this to the career and present prospects of Edward Boyce, who less than ten years ago had been initiated by Tom Crabbice into the habits of those haunts of dissipation and vice with which Tom himself had, even then, become perfectly familiar. The one now holds up his head in the best society of the place, the other is looked upon by all his old associates as a degraded 'fallen' man.

How shall we account for it? Was the saying, that as a man soweth, so shall he reap, true in the one case, and a mere figure of speech in the other? Was it the case that Tom Crabbice had sown wild oats and was now to reap full-eared golden grain—that though both had sown the wind, Edward Boyce alone was to 'fill his bosom' with the whirlwind?

Ask that broken-hearted wife, as she sits in her cheerless home, the head and husband of which has been rendered a terror and affliction to his own, through that man's evil companionship, whether *she* can believe it? Ask those young women against whom the finger of scorn is pointed, and upon whom is the brand of infamy, whether they think it possible that the seducer of innocence, the destroyer of their good name, can escape the retribution which their wild and frantic prayers invoke upon his head?

Meanwhile all this is unseen and unheard of by 'the world', as Thomas Crabbice, Esq., knows it, and desires to be known by it. He is a strict, punctual business man, so reputed, and so desiring to be reputed. And having identified himself with certain benevolent 'causes', whose orthodoxy is unimpeachable, the comfortable and well-to-do world will not look too minutely after his acts, even should he advance 'sharp practice' to the dignity of a maxim in his business operations, take full advantage of the power his wealth gives him to drive an unfair bargain with the poor trader; or deal as ruthlessly as he chooses with the man who owes him money, and finds himself in the unfortunate position of being unable to pay it with the promptitude which is in accordance with exact business habits. And what though his constitution, mental and moral, as well as physical, should be of the texture of the soundest leather. It has this advantage, that it can as yet, at least, retain within it, without the slightest symptom of straining, those eternal elements of woe, which in a constitution less outwardly fenced, and with more of the action of the human heart within, would have burst their temporary confinement and been doing their wild and baleful work long ago.

One of the last things that Patrick Crabbice, Esq., had done in the shape of business, was to give certain instructions to his agent anent poinding for rent, and 'account due', the furniture of a worthless tenant. The old man's death stayed the operation for a little; but of course business is business, and even death must not stay it, or the world would come to a stand still. 'Oh; yes, yes, Mr. Sharkey,' said Mr. Thomas Crabbice to his law agent, 'That Ross is a worthless fellow—you'll better go on with the poinding.'

'I believe his wife's ill, Sir. They've had fever in their family.'

'Oh! there's for ever some excuse. The woman's quite able to be remov't, I believe; and, as there's a chance of letting the house to another, ye'll better just put the warrant in execution. The place is gettin' disgraceful; there'll be nothing to pay rent nor anthing else very soon.'

And so George Ross had forthwith to quit his 'premises', at 30, Batter Lane, and seek shelter for his household where he could find it. The companion picture was found in poor Edward Boyce, roused for once to a righteous indignation, ransacking his now but badly replenished purse, and pledging his sadly waning credit, to provide for him a new 'home'—if the sacred name may be so desecrated; for George Ross was simply removed to another lane of a similar character; into another house, a *fac simile* of that he was leaving, to pursue the same degrading business. Alas, he now was, and for years had been, fit for no other and better.

Chapter XXXII

ROBERT MORRIS AT HOME

To Mrs. Morris the evening of her son's return home was a peculiarly happy one. He had been but two weeks absent, yet that was an unwonted thing. Then Mrs. Morris expected to obtain no end of information as to the places he had visited, the sights he had seen, and the deeds he had done. But a mother in the fulness of her joy and love even, is not selfish. Here are you now with all your pretensions to generous and unselfish feeling—Are there not those dear to you, all whose presence when you meet, after separation, you would wish to claim as your own literally and exclusively; and perhaps, if you could have it your own way, for no limited period of time, either? Yet who is dearer to you than that plain, prosaic son to the mother, who on his return, like the woman that had found the 'lost piece of silver', and called 'her neighbours and friends' to rejoice with her, invites others to be sharers in the calm, deep joy she feels. And thus had Mrs. Morris expressly asked James Munro to meet Robert on the night of his return.

James arrived promptly, for he wished to be at the train to meet his friend. 'And of course you go with me, Lizzie' was his remark to Miss Morris.

'Don't you think that style o' addressing a young lady rude enough to deter me, Mr. Munro?' was the reply.

'Rude? Well, perhaps, takin' the mere words an' measurin' them by the conventional standard o' politeness. But will you tell me that in manner or spirit, the mode of address was rude?'

'Didn't I say something unco like it?'

'No; none of your evasions now, my sma' woman. You might take my words in their literality, and say, that was a rude, unpolite form of address. And I might take the bare words o' your first question and say, that your reply was querulous and pettish, and we should baith be fools for our pains. So you see there's something mair in courtesy than bare words, Lizzie.'

'An' isn't it a mercy for some folk that it is so?' asked Lizzie slyly.

'I suppose you mean to be personal now, my worthy damoiselle, but I've a comfortably thick hide in sick-like matters; so begone your gate.' And the two went forth together, with certainly no appearance of any lack of mutual confidence.

Had Robert Morris been a witness of this small colloquy it might have tended so far to relieve his mind of a certain peculiar feeling in connection with his friend which had been rather growing of late, and at which he felt thoroughly vexed. It was that feeling, which somewhat later in the evening, helped to make Robert almost perceptibly start, and quite perceptibly colour to the top of his brows, when his mother, among other queries about his travels, asked with much innocence—

'An' did you see Agnes Wilson, Robert?'

'Yes, mother, I did. What put it in your head to ask that question?' was the answer hurriedly stammered out.

'I though you would call on *her* at any rate,' said Mrs. Morris. The truth was the worthy woman's notions of the geography of the British Empire were not very exact; and so knowing the fact that her son was going to the north of England, and knowing also that Agnes Wilson was living in the north of England, she concluded that his visiting her was a result as certain as a call from Johnnie Duncan at her own house in the north quarter of Strathaven was an unfailing result of Johnnie having occasion to honour that part of the burgh with his presence. Robert, somewhat disconcerted as he was, could not help feeling that he had better be explicit at once—'in for a penny in for a pound'—and so he added.

'Aye, mother, I saw Agnes. An' what do you think—I went fifty miles out o' my way for the purpose of seeing her?'

'I would have done that too. How is she?'

'She is well, and cheerful as usual; and, as usual, had much to ask about you.'

'Agnes is a good girl, Robert. They used to say hoo lucky Elsie Graham was by her, to get so weel married; but hoo much better is she noo, though she should never marry!'

'Perhaps she never will,' said Robert.

'Never marry; what makes you think that?'

'Oh, I don't mean to say *that*, mother,' answered Robert laughing, 'I know nothing about it'; then hastily turning the conversation, he asked how Mrs. Boyce's health was.

'She's much worse than before,' said Lizzie, 'She hasna been able to be much oot o' bed since ye left. An' it's so sad—Mr. Boyce mad wi' drink every ither night; either drinkin' at hame wi' that miserable creature, Lillie, whom he now takes to his ain house, or comin' hame staggerin', and ready to quarrel wi' the very servan', who has waited to let him in and help him to bed.'

'An' there's a message doon that she wants to see you as soon as ye can, Robert,' added Mrs. Morris.

'Weel, mither, I'll go an' call to-morrow; though I believe Edward Boyce has nae wish to see me noo at his ain house, or elsewhere.'

'What a pitiful, wretched course that man is runnin',' said James Munro. 'There must be something viciously weak—a terrible lack o' moral stamina—in his character, before he could so utterly disregard a' that appeals most strongly to his natural affections; an' also fatuously see his vera property goin' to wreck before his een, without a single effort worthy o' a man, to recover himsel'.'

'Aye, aye, Jamie,' said Robert, shaking his head, 'but is he alone accountable. Had Edward Boyce not been led on imperceptibly to acquire a diseased, but irresistible craving for strong drink, which, while it was sapping his constitution mental and physical, was gradually stimulatin' the terrible desire, and weakenin' the power to resist it, what might not have been made of his open, generous nature? What a curse must rest on the responsible means of his ruin. He was once one of my best friends,' added Robert warmly.

'Weary, wretched drink!' responded Mrs. Morris.

'No!' interrupted Robert, with unwonted vehemence, 'we maunna be so silly as to lay our feeble anathemas on mere material substances; think rather o' the conscious human will that is not content with perilling its own best interests, but will o' set purpose draw on others in the downward path. Think o' their responsibility, who are not content wi' turnin' the gift of God into a form that has power to madden the brain, enslave the intellect, an' inflame the brute passions o' their fellowmen, but also use every inducement in their power to make them partake o' the unblest draught.'

'That's something unco like a high-flown total abstinence speech, Robbie; but rather than start an argument wi' you the nicht, we would hear some further account o' yer travels.'

Some further account of his travels was given accordingly, Robert, nothwithstanding his efforts to the contrary, manifesting a slight embarrassment whenever his mother referred, as she once or twice again, in the simplicity of her heart did, to the part of the journey where Agnes Wilson came in. When the hour of parting came, and the two young men were alone, James Munro turned to his friend and somewhat abruptly exclaimed, 'Noo, Robbie, I've been wont to look on you as the wise experienced man, an' mysel' as the halloch, hairbrain't fool. But some o' yer appearances of late, an' the nicht in particular, would almost lead me to believe that our positions are just about the reverse.'

'Very complimentary, no doubt!'

Never min', if it's true. We've twa three things else besides compliments to realise in the course of our personal history, as ye may know.'

'An' I daresay I do,' said Robert, half sadly.

'Well, but the bounds of human experience are ill to reach; yet experience does teach a lesson or two not otherwise so readily to be acquired. Know then, Mr. Robert, that I have marked, and thoroughly comprehend your feeling towards a young woman, whose name has been mentioned oftener than once this night. I know she is worthy o' your respect, your most devoted love—if you choose—worthy of the latter because entitled to the former. So then, my good friend, let no jealousy of any other man disturb your thoughts—least o' a', jealousy of your humble servant——'

'Come, come, Jamie, are ye in earnest, now?' stammered Robert.

'Weel, I've about learn't to give up weak sentimentality on such subjects, at least. You once put to me the question, whether a certain reference had a personal application. My answer was postponed; an' without sayin' whether it is given noo or no, there are some sharp and bitter lessons taught us, it may be, which we would be a little more than fools to invite a repetition of. And so while a second affection, true and entire, *may* fill the place of the first where you have loved, "not wisely but too well", those who form it will be sadly left to themselves if they make not sure of their ground long before they can be in a position to discover that—they have trusted all, and all is lost!'

'James, it would be worse than hypocrisy to deny to you that I do love Agnes Wilson; but if she regards you more, and you——'

'Stop there, young man, believe me you need have no fear as to who she regards. For me, dear Robbie—shall I confess it—I've openly wooed and won your good sister, Lizzie, under your own unsuspecting eyes! An' mair than that, I was just cogitating how best to break the tale to you, when *your* embarrassment sent my ain fairly to flight.'

Chapter XXXIII

A MURDER—IS IT?

'This is a terrible bizziness, Mr. Morris! I was aye thinkin' something wud happen o' a gruesome kin.'

'What has happened Johnnie?'

'Oh hinna ye heard o' the murder?'

'Murder! What do you mean?'

'Lillie, ye ken. That peer drucken doitet lawyer bodie—gotten dead this mornin' i' the ditch, no abeen a quarter o' a mile farrer on—his skull clown in twa, an's harns driven throu the back o't.'

'Gotten murdered in the ditch?'

'Aye, aye; an' my certy may weel seem to be. There's as muckle bleed i' the ditch yet as though ye had sticket a sheep.'

'Why, Johnnie, how has this come aboot?'

'Weel, Sir, I'm thinkin' fae fat I heard i' the toon—dinna say 't I taul ye, Mr. Morris, though—that it had been in Geordie Ross's they had been drinkin' last nicht. An' some starshie had ta'en place gaen hame—an' he had cuttit's craig wi' a jockteleg knife an' thrown him intill the ditch.'

'He? Who had done that?'

'Oh bless ye I forgat ye hedna heard,' and Johnnie Duncan lowered his voice to a whisper almost.

'It's the laird they're blamin' for 't.'

'Tut, Johnnie, he would surely be the last man. Ye mustna mention sick a thing.'

'Weel, weel, I'se be but owre glaid if he's clear't o't, peer lad. Onyhoo Lillie was gotten there this mornin' a caul stiff corp.'

'An' who discover't the body.'

'On it was some cairter lads gaun awa to drive trees fae the Hill. The foremost naig ye see fley't at it it i' the grey daylicht an' so they gat the polees an' they're makin' a full interrogation o' the whole circumferences ye ken.'

Robert Morris was on his way from his mother's cottage to his office on the morning after we last parted with him when he met Johnny Duncan, who had been at Strathaven, and with his usual unction gave him the foregoing details relative to Mr. Daniel Lillie; and which in the main proved to be correct—with of course the usual allowance for embellishment in narration.

Lillie had been found that morning dead in the ditch by the roadside, a short way out of Strathaven. The body was not mutilated to quite the extent indicated by the beadle, but there were some abrasions and a slight cut or two about the head. It was known that after an uproarious evening at George Ross's whisky shop, along with other tipsy and half-tipsy men, Lillie and Edward Boyce had left together at a late hour on the previous night. Subsequently to this, Lillie had not been seen again in life—not seen at all, till found a livid corpse in the ditch.

As he proceeded into the town, Robert Morris found Strathaven all astir with the exciting news, of a probable, or, at any rate, possible murder. He went on quietly to the special scene of his labours, received hearty welcome back from Mr. Patten, the senior partner, and the small boy and porter who represented the officials of the firm. The conclusion, and a not unnatural one, at which Robert had arrived, was that Lillie, in one of his drunken fits, had missed his footing and fallen into the ditch, and, in absence of internal vigour or external aid, had lain still, and died where he lay. It was therefore with a measure of surprise, as well as deep pain, he heard, in course of a few hours, that Edward Boyce had actually been brought to Strathaven in charge of the police, who believed they had the strongest 'presumptions' against him as the murderer of Daniel Lillie.

Sad and painful beyond expression as the duty was in the circumstances, Robert Morris felt he might not shrink from visiting Mrs. Boyce on that very day. If he meant to do so before what had transpired only made the call doubly imperative. He found her feebler in health; indeed, quite unable to leave her room, but calm and self-possessed, to a degree that quite surprised him. Her woman's quickness had enabled her at once to perceive the constraint and embarrassment of Robert, who was uncertain whether she knew anything, or how much of that morning's revelations—and after the first few words of mutual salutation and inquiry, she at once put an end to all reserve by saying—

'I know all, Mr. Morris. You are astonished at my calmness. But on this earth now I have nothing to hope or dread from him. Edward had fallen farther than perhaps even you had dreamt of. His hands have struck me; *his* feet have kicked my poor body! For me there was nothing worse; for himself, alas! what *could* be worse than what I have seen and known for months on months; *my* Edward, associating with the vilest men and the vilest women in this place. I know he is not guilty of killing that poor, wretched man. No; never! Deep and deadly as the injury is which that creature had helped to inflict on him, Edward would never have injured a hair of his head. Yet, if they would take him and confine him, away from all such, hard as it might be, what were it but a blessing to himself, compared to what has been?

'I believe with you,' said Robert Morris, 'that he is not guilty of that charge. Would that the very fact of its being made could make him reflect, and turn from that which has been his undoing. Would it were possible, if only for your sake and not his own alone.'

'Speak not of my sake,' said Mrs. Boyce. 'I feel and know that but a few weeks or months now will see me past such cares and trials. What a life mine has been! To you, who know all, I need not say how my early days were saddened—how many bitter tears I wept in secret for my poor dear father. Yet we saw not where the root of bitterest evil lay. We scouted the only means of safety for him—that was abjuring for ever the terrible snare by which he was led captive at Satan's will. And so it was with Edward. I see it now. I know it too late—in entire abstinence alone is there safety for him. With such as Edward the cursed thing works out its work speedily; yet are they better who carry its blighting influence in their bosoms to the close of a longer life than his can be?'

Robert Morris looked on with astonishment at hearing such sentiments, and the lady gazing at him with an earnestness that seemed impossible to her nature, as he had had hitherto understood it, proceeded—

'You are surprised, Mr. Morris, to hear me speak thus. I have at last learned through bitter, bitter experience what you told me long ago, though I gave but little heed to what you said. And now that my time is fast wearing out under the shadow of a terrible cloud, I wish you to promise that you will take what interest you can in my poor child. Oh, Mr. Morris, it is the thought of leaving her, and that alone, that makes death look gloomy. But I know you will befriend her. I have written to Agnes Wilson last night, to ask of her a similar promise—would that she lived near her.'

Robert Morris made the required promise, and thereafter closed the sad interview, musing, as he wended his way homeward, on the singular fact that he too had written Agnes Wilson on the previous night—a foolish and imprudent proceeding, he had hardly dared to doubt, even while in the very act of carrying it out—and which, as coming in close connection with matters of such grave and painful import, he now mentally condemned as something wearing a very selfish and ill-timed aspect.

Chapter XXXIV

THE SMIDDY

It would have been extremely ungenerous to detract by one iota from the honour and glory justly due to the Beadle, in being the first to carry the tidings of the murder of Daniel Lillie to the Kirktown. On Johnnie's prompt return thither, after that melancholy event, the scene in King John anent 'young Arthur's death' was literally repeated—almost. We don't mean to say that 'five moons' had been seen, nor even four; yet putting the beadle's story in place of such portent, it might be truly said—

> Old men and beldams in the streets.
> Do prophesy upon it dangerously.
> .   .   .   .
>
> And when they talk of him they shake their heads,
> And whisper one another in the ear,
> And he that speaks doth gripe the hearer's wrist;
> Whilst he that hears makes fearful action,
> With wrinkled brows, with nods, with rolling eyes.

But we had better not add—

> I saw a smith stand with his hammer, thus,
> The whilst his iron did on the anvil cool,
> With open mouth swallowing a tailor's news.

Johnnie Duncan, indeed, felt that this was no ordinary bit of gossip wherewith one might gratify and astonish silly women alone, but a great and horrible narration, fit to ring in the sturdiest masculine ears. So in place of seeking the society of Mrs.

Muggart and her friends first, he rehearsed the matter in the ears of sundry out-door auditors, whom he encountered, some in groups, some singly, and some of whom he had never even spoken to before. Then under a somewhat mistaken impulse— Shakespeare notwithstanding—he wended his way along Cooms Causeway to the smiddy of the Kirktown, where, in addition to the smith, the smith's man, and a few ordinary loungers about the place, he found our old acquaintance, Mr. Pattle of Gouckstyle, down for the purpose of getting a pair of cart wheels 'ringed' by the smith. Ringing wheels was an important operation. The smith had none of your modern machinery for the purpose, but bent his rings by dint of the 'strong fore hammer', on a big stone hollowed on its upper side, which stood by the door cheek. And then when the great business of heating the ring before putting it on came, the 'hearth' was cleared, the furnace heated seven times, and a bed of 'shealin' sids' laid all round for the ring to ignite, as it was gradually shoved round by the long nosed tongs, in order to keep up its own heat. The smith, a prime, rough, sturdy looking chiel, with his head clipped wonderfully bare, stripped to the shirt and trousers, and with bare, brawny arms, worked the bellows with a steady, powerful sweep. This was the presiding genius of the place; a man whose sole weakness—attributable perhaps to the nature of his occupation—was a perennial thirst, as if a live cinder had really stuck in his throat—and the smith did not always quench it with the most cooling liquids. And thus was he occupied when Johnnie Duncan, with an air of proper consequence, stepped into the smiddy. The smith was, perhaps, not exactly quite cool, but quite collected at least, so, on seeing Johnnie enter, he roared out

'Weel, bellman, fat's ye're news the day?'

Johnnie required a prefatory hem or two to 'redd his craig' for the stunning announcement, but ere it came the smith, who had no excess of courtesy in general, nor of respect toward the beadle in particular, had turned round to poke up his fire, and seemed in no hurry to withdraw his attention from his own proper business again.

This was rather more than Johnnie's patience could stand, and he had begun his tale to the others who stood in the smiddy floor, when Gouckstyle who had also 'casten' his coat, and had just returned with a 'fraucht o' water' in readiness for the ringing, entered.

'Fat sorra's this ye're haverin' at noo min?' was the salutation of Mr. Pattle to the excellent beadle.

'I'll tell ye fat it is Maister Pattle—that's nae the gate to speak to nae man on sic an occasion,' answered Johnnie with dignity.

'Ou nae,' replied Gouckstyle, 'an' fat for no. I sud like to ken fa has ony gryte cause to be sorry at the loss o' a peer drucken never-do-weel. Fat mair likely nor 't *he* sud come by's deeth in a ditch some day?'

'Deed there wus greater losses at Culloden I suppose,' said the smith, who now with his back to the hearth, and the fire in capital trim, stood taking a long and leisurely stroke at the bellows. And as he liked to illustrate a point clearly, he added—'aye wus there; as the laddie said 't lost "his fader an's breeder an' a gweed buff-belt weel worth them baith". But fat's this ye wus sayin' aboot the laird bein' ta'en up for't, Johnnie?'

'A weel, gin a body cud get in their word, or be trate wi' ordinar civeelity—I was jist sayin' 't there's a very strong surmise 't he's hed something adee wi't, an' the polees are awa at this vera time to comprehen' 'im.'

'Nonsense min,' again interrupted the impetuous Gouckstyle, 'That's conter to rizzon to beleive 't the laird wud a tribblet a hair o's heed.'

'Weel, weel,' answered Johnnie, justly nettled at the way in which the effect of his tidings was being marred, 'I'm only tellin' ye the facks o' the maitter—that 'll stan' law ony day.'

'That kin' o' clypes gedder aye feet as they gae; an' I'se warran' this ane's lost naething on the road up fae Strathaven,' said Gouckstyle drily.

'Weel boys the ring's jist na'ar het aneuch—see an' get oot the dogs there an' the fore-hemmers Sawney.'

The orders of 'Burnewin' must of course be obeyed; and so amid much heat and splutter, and sour reek of the burning felloes, hissing of cold water on hot iron, sturdy 'yahissing' of the smith's Sawney with the forehammer on the edge of the 'ring', and the stentorian commands of the smith now to give 'Water'—which Gouckstyle, with the aid of the smith's wife's tea kettle, did as promptly and exactly as the abounding reek would let him—and now to 'Chap! Chap!'—the wheels were 'rung', first one and then the other. And they drank a dram 'on the heeds o't', for Mr. Pattle was not so neglectful nor so shabby as to fail to bring a bottle of real mountain dew in his pocket.

It is needless to say that long before this Johnnie Duncan had sought a more sympathetic audience to whom he might narrate *in extenso*. And he found it in the souter's shop, where both the active operator, and the congenial onlookers have always more leisure and more breath for long-winded gossiping than can be expected in the smiddy, at any rate in the crisis of such operations as ringing wheels, or shoeing a 'flingin' mare that needs the 'lip-girn' to bring her to reason.

That Johnnie's story was better worth listening to than they had supposed, even the smith and Gouckstyle found out by and bye. Edward Boyce had not only been apprehended, but after the usual preliminary investigation, taken before the Sheriff to make his Declaration. By Robert Morris's intervention, a respectable lawyer had been got to attend to his case. He admitted at once having been in the company of Lillie, up to a late hour on the evening previous to his being found dead; as also that they left the public house together, but so confused was his recollection of what occurred after this, that on being warned in the usual way that anything he might say would be used against him on his trial, he, by his agent's instructions, declined to make any explanatory declaration. And so he was 'committed for trial'.

This latter fact became known to the beadle quite promptly. For, why, the jailor of Strathaven was the beadle's own particular friend. One of his greatest achievements indeed, in the line of his own profession had been that of making down a suit of the 'jiler's' uniform for family purposes. The 'jiler' was a spare brawny man, and it required no small extent of cloth to cover him, as the result in this case well testified. For the beadle by dint of superior contrivance manufactured out of the uniform a whole 'stan' o' blue' to the jiler's aul'est loon; also a pair of queetikins to the jiler himself, and a specially grand blue bonnet, which had a bit 'snout', while the crown was wide and baggy, with seams running from the big button in the centre toward the circumference (after the manner of the sun in his glory painted in bold lines on a tavern signboard). And besides all this there were remnants sufficient to supply the jiler's wife with almost the entire material of a 'clouty carpet'.

The jiler wore his bonnet and queetikins on grand undress occasions. No wonder that he and the beadle were fast friends. And as little wonder that, in virtue of his daily visit to the jiler and confab with him after the poor laird's incarceration, and while he waited the sitting of the Circuit Court, Johnnie should be the 'local authority' undisputed on all the particulars and probabilities of the sad case. Of course Johnnie received his information in strict confidence—a confidence he would not have violated for 'wardle's gear'. Still you know the expectant gossip found his society worth cultivating; and, indeed, Johnnie knew that the general public of the Kirktown looked upon him as a greater man than ever. And he was very gracious and condescending to the public, only he never risked another visit to the Smiddy.

Chapter XXXV

THE STRATHAVEN POST-OFFICE

Rory Mactaggart, postmaster of Strathaven, was a queer 'little mannie', who wore a suit of rusty black, and a hat immensely too big for his head, and still more out of proportion to the size of his body; it was, too, perpetually stuffed with papers of various kinds, and gave him the appearance of being top-heavy. He took snuff liberally from a worn silver box, 'the gift of friends', in some past period of his life, and his shrivelled face betokened fully as much cunning as any other quality. The Postmaster's fortune had been various. As a member of a family of local position, he had gone abroad in his youth; how he did in foreign countries was not particularly known. At least, it was kept a family secret, unless in so far as the gossips of Strathaven had stories, partly founded on fact perhaps, partly theoretical, of his vicious ill-doing. Anyhow, he returned without having reached the dignity of a millionaire—the original intent when he started. He next drew upon his friends, again settled down in business in Strathaven, a somewhat experienced man of the world; and in due course became bankrupt, presented a very bad 'state of affairs', made up with scrupulous minuteness, to his creditors, paid them 1s 7½d in the pound, and started once more, nothing abashed, and bating no jot of heart or hope. With this process he became, indeed, somewhat familiar, his bankruptcies having numbered three or four in all; for when he had incurred debts to a respectable amount, if he could not shuffle out of them by one or other of the dodges patent to an acute pettifogger, why he called a halt, got sequestration, wiped off the old score and began anew. And all the while he enjoyed life—that is, took snuff all day, and drank toddy every evening, talked local politics, and local scandal and obscenity—with a zest which no man who endeavoured to pay his just and lawful debts could have exceeded, and very few equalled.

And thus, when the responsible public situation of postmaster became vacant, Rory having just newly got over a 'failure', of a rather more disastrous kind than usual even, became a candidate for it. There were a half-dozen other applicants of unimpeachable character and qualifications. But Rory was a man of family, and his wife had 'influential connections', and so, with the nice discrimination of merit which usually obtains when such influences come into play, the appointment was bestowed upon him, to the intense satisfaction of those highly respectable persons his relatives, who were getting to be somewhat at a loss what to do with Rory next.

He did his postmaster business after his own fashion. Among a certain class of H.M. officials in this line, who have not a large amount of the correspondence of the public passing through their hands, a portion of the spare time at command is zealously devoted to scrutinising the exterior, at least, of certain of the letters going outward or inward; and the postmaster (or mistress) and his cronies hazard a variety of conjectures as to what is going on between the writers. Love affairs, for example; or some man receiving an epistle of legal and portentous aspect, implying that he at least is in a bad way. Considering the extent of the Strathaven postal business, it was surprising how closely Rory looked after this department. Had he been a mere roadside postmaster, with the box 'FOR UNPAID LETTERS' occupying the biggest pane in his dingy window, and two or three glass jars filled of peppermint lozenges in the remaining available space, he could hardly have taken more exact note of what was going on. And then he had a free and easy habit of every now and then allowing letters to drop aside for a day or two before they were delivered, or despatched, as the case might be.

It was because Rory did a certain thing of this latter sort on a certain occasion that we have thus imperfectly sketched the 'wile bodie'.

Away in her English home, Agnes Wilson had received a letter from Strathaven, and was shocked and grieved in no ordinary

degree, to find the main burden of its contents to be an announcement of the miserable predicament into which Edward Boyce, in
one of his mad fits of drunkenness, had got himself anent the
matter of Daniel Lillie. 'I felt I could not delay writing you thus
soon again, lest you might receive an exaggerated account of
what is bad enough at best, but from which I hope some good,
that we cannot yet see, may ultimately come.' So said the writer
of the letter in drawing the story to a close; and then added, by
way of P.S.:

> MY DEAR MISS WILSON,—If you can do no more, at least
> pardon me for writing you, as I have at last done. It may have
> been unwise in one like myself to cherish such feelings, or give
> expression to such sentiments. Yet it was no mere impulse of
> the moment. Ever since I gazed in your calm, peaceful eyes
> at Strathaven manse, on an occasion which I shall never
> forget, I have somehow felt that it *must* be so. And be it wise,
> or very foolish in the eyes of others, my unbounded faith in
> your good sense gives me the fullest assurance that you can
> overlook defects on my part that would be but too obvious to
> others.

'"Such feelings", and "such sentiments", and "unbounded
faith"—"What next, and next?"' thought Agnes, who, if
startled by the epistle itself, was little short of astounded by the
postscript—'Has Robert Morris too gone daft? He who had such
a reputation for sober common sense and discretion; whom one
might lean upon so securely amid any of life's trials and changes,
certain that they would find him ever at heart the same—stead-
fast, unselfish and unswerving!' Agnes read the postscript again
and again, with a puzzled look; and there, up in that solitary little
room in the great house, which was called her own, she sat and
mused all alone, with the letter in her lap, till the gathering dusk
of a raw spring evening had deepened into thick gloom, and the
want of fire made her feel chilled and stiff. And then like a sensible woman, as she really was, she prepared herself to go to bed.
What Agnes's thoughts were, or whether any light as to the
mysterious postscript had dawned on her mind I know not.

Next morning Agnes was down stairs betimes to ask if the postman had yet called on his early round, 'Yes 'm, and a letter for
you', was the smart flunkey's reply. And that odd presentiment

that so it would be, was fulfilled, for it was a letter from
Strathaven. What its contents were I can't say; and what Agnes's
reply was I won't give any indication whatever. I am only bound
to explain that through the eccentricities of Rory Mactaggart's
mode of postal despatch, the letter that Robert Morris wrote
informing Agnes Wilson of Daniel Lillie's decease, and its
accompaniments, had been sent on towards its destination a day
sooner than a certain other letter written by the same person to
'the same address', and posted on the previous night. And it is
a matter of fair inference, I presume, that the text of the epistle
last-mentioned would throw some light on the perplexing postscript of the other which had been penned subsequent to it; and
which certainly would not fit on well to a circumstantial account
of the deplorable death of the defunct Strathaven solicitor.

Chapter XXXVI

NOT PROVEN

The Spring Circuit of Justiciary, or what our Southern neighbours would call the Assizes, of 185—had a pretty heavy calendar of crime from Strathaven. A case of petty forgery, four or five thefts, aggravated by the perpetrators of them being 'habit and repute, and previously convicted thieves', and a charge of murder. The Court-house was crowded to suffocation when the principal case was called, and there stepped up into the prisoner's dock, by a sliding trap-door that conducted from a lower region of prison cells, a pale, haggard-looking man, with but little of the aspect of the habitual criminal, and some remains yet of the 'gentlemanlike' in his bearing.

'Edward Boyce—you are charged with the murder of Daniel Lillie; what say you? Are you guilty or not guilty?' asked one of the bewigged Judges on the Bench.

'Not guilty, my Lord,' was the answer, and the prisoner sat down with the air of one perfectly lost to hope, and indifferent to his fate. The Clerk of Court proceeded to select a Jury to try the case. Among the names on whom the lot fell, and which were shouted out by the Clerk, was that of 'Thomas Crabbice of Vatville'. A prompt 'Here' was the response, and the proprietor of Vatville rose, hat in hand, with a business-like air, to push his way to the Jury box. At this announcement of his name, there were sudden whisperings among some of the spectators, the prisoner started to a more erect position, and his eye lighted up as he leant forward to speak to his counsel—an eminent member of the Scotch bar. 'I object', said the learned gentleman across the table, and the Clerk again shouted out, 'You may keep your seat, Mr. Crabbice'. Mr. C. bowed with the air of a man who knew the majesty of the law and respected it, the prisoner once more sunk back to his former listless position, and the selection of the jury proceeded.

The trial went on as such trials do. Witnesses were at once called by the public prosecutor, to prove the charge. After one or two official gentlemen had been examined, chiefly for identification of documents, and to show that the case had been formally conducted hitherto, there stepped into the witness-box a dull looking man, whose face spoke of little but strong drink, and his habiliments of little but dirt and sloth.

'George Ross, number 6, my lord,' exclaimed the red-nosed Macer. George was duly sworn, and detailed how the prisoner and the deceased had spent the evening together in his house, the night before Daniel Lillie was found by the roadside dead.

'They were not tipsy. Yes; they had some drink o' coorse durin' the evenin'. No a great quantity. Couldna say hoo much exactly.' 'Tell us as near as you can?' queried the Advocate-Depute. 'Couldna say exactly' was repeated. 'Was there a gill or five gills, or a gallon?' 'Na; they got it in half mutchkins.' 'How many?' 'Cudna say; Maister Boyce paid for twa or three. Yes, there was a company along wi' them. They were a' perfectly sober.' 'And quiet?' 'Yes; as quate as usual. There was several women as well as men—some o' them married women, and some o' them unmarried, I suppose. There was some o' them dancin'. Yes; the prisoner at the bar danced wi' some of the women, an' at anither time he was whistlin' a tune to them and knackin' his thooms. I don't consider such proceedings unruly. The parties seemed to be enjoyin' themselves. An' Maister Boyce was very cheery wi' them a'. They warna quarrelsome. I dinna consider cursin' and swearin' anything beyond ordinary. No; I don't approve of such practices in my house. Yes; I mean to say they are nothing extraordinary in a public house.'

The evidence, in short, amounted to this—that after an evening spent in the way described, Edward Boyce and Lillie had left together, as usual; and nothing more had been seen of them that night, nor until Lillie was found a corpse in a ditch, as already described, and Edward Boyce got by the police in his bed at Drammochdyle at mid-day, sleeping off the effects of the debauch. Near where Lillie's body lay there were footprints that appeared to indicate a struggle, but they were not so distinctly marked as to prove that Edward Boyce had actually been there. Lillie's injuries consisted, as has been stated, of a cut about the temples, and some abrasions; the former looked as if made by a pocket knife, of not particularly keen edge, an instrument which Edward Boyce was known to have possessed recently, but of which no trace could be found now. Putting these circumstances in their fullest force against the prisoner formed the case for the prosecution.

In defence, a clever medical man set up the theory (which a less clever professional brother corroborated) that Lillie, while in a state of intoxication, as the evidence showed that he must have been, had slipped and stumbled into the ditch; and that the cut on his brow was inflicted by the edge of a sharp, projecting stone in the hard bank. And, at the request of the judges, the clever medical man knelt down in Court and jammed his own forehead against a bench, to show how his theory could be carried into practice.

The clever counsel for the accused too—one who could recollect Edward Boyce as a college companion though he gave no indication of *that* either by word or look—badgered some rather astute official witnesses terribly about their getting up of the case, and in his address to the 'gentlemen of the jury' made a very strong point of the want of motive for such a deed, on the part of the prisoner. How was it possible to believe that *he* could have murdered the very man who in the 'winter of his fortune' was his chief bosom friend, and with whom he had never been known to pass an angry word? Then with respect to the medical evidence, what more probable than that the eminent witnesses he had called had suggested the exact mode of this unfortunate man's death. The medical witnesses for the crown had been unable to do more than give a dry enumeration of the appearance of various marks on the corpse, which read like the page of a technical dictionary, and could not positively assert that any lethal weapon whatever had been used against the deceased; while he had been able to put before them a theory rationally accounting for these wounds—mere scratches—and which bore the strongest evidence of probability in the face of it. Then he needed not to remind them of the state in which the blood of a habitual drunkard is, nor remind them how readily a cut of this sort, which a healthy man could afford to regard as a mere scratch, might prove fatal to a man, the fluids of whose body were vitiated by constant excess in spirituous liquor, as was but too clearly the case with this unfortunate man. He claimed a verdict of acquittal at the hands of an intelligent and impartial jury.

The result of the trial was that the intelligent jury, after consultation for an hour or two, took refuge in the grand safety valve of the Scottish judicature, and returned a verdict of 'Not proven'.

And so Edward Boyce left the bar again—a free man—shall we say? But ere he was well outside of the court-house, there were some of his old companions ready to meet and greet him—to offer congratulations, and to express friendship in their own way.

It had been Robert Morris's intention to endeavour to meet him and prevent any such risk. Yet, though it was doubtless a false delicacy, he had strong notions of the individual's personal freedom, and could not prevent the thought rising 'What right have I to constitute myself his protector, and thrust myself forward upon him impertinently'. And so while he waited for the fit and natural opportunity the chance of its coming was destroyed by others as well as the chance of Edward Boyce returning direct to his home which Robert fain hoped he would do.

That very night Edward Boyce returned to Drammochdyle, if not drunk, yet strongly excited by drink.

Chapter XXXVII

A LAST LOOK AT DRAMMOCHDYLE

During the time that Edward Boyce lay in jail his wife had been getting gradually weaker, and by the time he was once more at liberty she was altogether confined to bed. Their first meeting on his return from the assizes was painful in the extreme. Half tipsy as he was, he felt dreadfully put out at the thought of going into her presence. And when with faltering steps and heart ill at ease he approached her bedside and saw the poor wasted figure before him, and for the first time realised his wife's real condition, he felt at last indeed that he *was* a condemned criminal. And as he seized her thin, worn hand, the poor infatuated man burst into tears and cried like a child.

'Oh Edward, Edward! why thus again' murmured the dying woman as her husband bent over to kiss her.

'Elsie, dearest; don't reproach me now.'

'Reproach you, Edward?—God knows I do not; but why destroy yourself?'

'Oh Elsie, Elsie, what shall I do—you must get better.'

'Edward,' was the calm, earnest response, 'I am dying. I will soon be "where the wicked cease from troubling, and where the weary be at rest." But oh let me entreat you, by all that is sacred; by all that we have both known—to fly from this terrible fate— the drunkard's doom!'

'I cannot—I dare not—I have brought Heaven's curse upon my own head. There is no hope,' exclaimed the miserable man.

The arrival of the doctor put an end to the painful scene. He simply bowed to Mr. Boyce, without speaking, and the latter, as conscious, even yet, that his presence as he then was was an outrage in the chamber of death, slunk to the door, and slowly, with piteous backward look, withdrew.

Edward Boyce never again saw his wife in the land of the living. That very night her spirit passed away—not without hope of a blessed resurrection—although her bed was watched only by hired attendants, while the husband for whom she had suffered so much lay steeped in the drunkard's heavy sleep. He attended the funeral, haggard and silent, and returned to the home amidst whose desolations his only remaining child, now a delicate looking girl of four years, wandered about and cried as if her heart would burst. Again and again he clasped her to his breast with a fervour that half frightened the unfortunate child; and then, wrapt in his own melancholy thoughts, wandered aimlessly about, now inside the house now out.

But things could not go on at Drammochdyle as they had been; and very soon Edward Boyce's creditors took steps to have his estate put under trustees.

Old Jeremiah Boyce's proposed entail had never been carried out; and we do not say that this was not now a convenience, so far, inasmuch as half the estate of Drammochdyle was quickly brought to the market and sold to satisfy his creditors. And Thomas Crabbice, Esq. of Vatville, now a leading man in the locality, reported to be on the eve of marriage to the daughter of a prominent county gentleman, added to his patrimonial estate by the purchase of this part of Drammochdyle. The other part was retained meanwhile, somewhat heavily burdened, the trustees making a pecuniary allowance to Edward Boyce.

Poor Edward had still enough left of the spirit of a man to feel his position. But alas! the terrible craving of his physical nature still remained, and that with the agony of his mind almost drove him to distraction; on his sadly abused intellect the thought seemed settling down that he was already amongst the reprobate —already in the place where hope is gone for ever. And in his wild ravings he would exclaim again and again, 'for me there is no hope—The devil will have me; he has me already'. But whatever thoughts rose he drowned, or tried to drown them in drink. Day after day he was drunk, often to great excess, and in proportion as he gave himself up to this habit did his violence grow while under the influence of drink, and his haggard gloom while at the opposite pole of his existence. He struck his servants, smashed the furniture, and occasionally wandered forth in a state of frantic excitement with little more than half his clothes on his person. He had literally become a terror to all about him; and as a last, and humane resort, application was made to the Procurator-Fiscal, by whom he was taken in charge, and under the Sheriff's warrant placed in the County Lunatic Asylum as 'a dangerous lunatic'.

Chapter XXXVIII

THE STORY IS ENDED

Our story is ended. In its issue for September 18th, 185—the *Strathaven Independent*, as part of the contents of a particular column interesting to old maids and gossips generally, amongst other events notable in the history of the human individual announced as follows:

'Married at Strathaven, on the 15th inst., by the Rev. Jonathan Longskreed, Robert Morris, to Agnes, only daughter of the late Richard Wilson.'

And so, as would appear, Agnes had arrived at the full bearing of a certain letter the oddly disjoined postscript to which had puzzled her so much when read as an antescript—at least, she had come to a pretty distinct comprehension of the sentiments of the writer of it. I have only my friend John Duncan's account of the marriage, which no doubt is quite correct, and which may be given as nearly as possible in his own words, premising that John had been employed as a waiter on the occasion, and was in remarkably good spirits while narrating—that is directly after he returned to the Kirktoon—In fact he was fully more voluble than ordinary.

'Ou aye, I kent o' the coortship lang, lang ago man; fan Robbie wus but a peer jiner lad workin' at the manse, in Dr. Graham's time—I thocht aye it wud come to something.'

'Nae doot, Johnnie—I never saw *you* far oot yet.'

'Catch me noo. ''A nod's as gweed's a wink, till a blin' horse'', ye ken. Aye, weel, weel; but comin' till particulars—Jamie Munro hed nae seener gi'en up 's projeck o' gaen awa' to the

Ingies again an' sattl't doon to tak' chairge o' the machine bizness at the foonry, nor he wud hae Lizzie. An' so *their* marriage cam' aff in a han' clap a twalmonth syne—he's a daft head-strong chiel, ye ken.'

'I dinna ken; but never min'.'

'Tak' my word for't than if ye dinna ken. So fan this affair cam' oot neist Mrs. Morris says to me, says she, "a wat Robbie's been a gweed son to me; an' Agnes's a perfeck jewel; but fat raiks Maister Duncan", says she?' 'As the aul' byeword says—

> My dother's my dother a' the days o' her life,
> An' my son's my son till he gets 'im a wife.'

So thinks Mrs. Morris, 'I canna bide langer wi' Robbie, for his wife *maun* be mistress in her ain hoose'—

'Tut, Johnnie, ye're wan'erin' fae the pint—I want to ken aboot the marriage itsel'.'

Heely, heely—hurry nae man's cattle—tak' things i' their naitral order. Weel, Jamie, he's been aye pressin' the aul' 'oman to gae an' live wi' them. "An' John", says she, "ye ken it's but naitral. It's an' ill wile't mither, and dother 't canna sort thegither".'

'I oonerstan' that Mrs. Morris is to live wi' her son-in-law—an' nae wi' her son?'

'Fat ither; wusna I tellin' ye? That 's the maist naitral arreengement; only she wuntit to tak' my advice observe ye. An' I'se warran' she's be a' the willin'er 't Lizzie's gotten a brow brat o' a bairnie the ither ouk'. An' Agnes she's boun' to tak' some chairge o' the laird's peer wee bit lassie.'

'Aye, aye; but bless us, Johnnie—fat o' the marriage? Keep yer little bits o' claivers o' that kin' for yer aul' wife gossips. Min' its no Mrs. Ellison an' the howdie yer speakin' till eenoo.'

'Dinna ye suppose 't I'm gaun to tell ye clypes oot o' the skweel noo, goodman. The marriage wus a vera quate, respectable pairty. There needs be no more said aboot it.'

John's dignity was evidently a little hurt.

'An' a weel conduckit, Mr. Duncan, fan ye wus in chairge, I'm sure. Ye've hed lairge experience in that way I'm weel awaar.'

'Ye may weel say't, laddie. There's no a man in Strathaven better up to the ettykit o' the thing. An' though I say't mysel',

there wusna a thing oot o' joint by a nail's bread', fae beginnin'
to en' o' the marriage.'

'An' fu did the bride luik?'

'Like a vera duchess—that 's no to say that she cuist a great
show, ye ken; for though she was aye a gey settin' deemie, she
wud a' never jist been my fancy for luik'—

'I cud weel believe *that*, John; for your Kirsten wi' her sonsy
braid shooders, bloomin' red cheeks, an' yellow hair, must hae
been a queenly luikin' 'oman at her best.'

'Aye, man, an' ye hed see Kirsten in her potestatur wi' her fite
muslin goon on—an' as mony red ribbons aboot her face as wud
'a set up a pack-merchan'.'

'Weel, fat did the bride wear—Agnes, I mean?'

'Ou deed, she had a dress o' some kin' o' lead colour't silk,
a white bonnet an' feathers in't—vera, vera nate—an' trimm't
wi' orange blossoms; an' a han'some Paisley shawl—vera genteel
she luikit I'll asseer ye. An' vera respectfu' wus she to me—'

'I cud never misdoot that John, but look here—There comes
yer nain Kirsten up the closs, and Mrs. Muggart wi' her, to get
the news, I fancy. I must go.'

'That wumman, Sir—she's a terrible claik. Mony's the affront
I've gotten wi' her lang ill guidet tongue.'

'John, John, ye mustna be ungallant.'

'Lat her keep her nain gate en' than, till she's wuntit.'

The door opened, and Johnnie adapted himself to circumstances. Kirsten, a remarkably hospitable and about equally
stupid woman, proceeded to bestow her motherly attentions on
the present writer. Johnnie exlaimed.

'Come awa', Mrs. Muggart. It's lang sin' we've seen ye.'

'Eh, na, John, I'm no comin' ben—ye've strangers wi' ye.'

'Tut, come awa, it's naebody in particler.'

'I *wudna* come, John, on nae account—nae for wardle's gear—
an' you upo' biziness. I hed nae erran' ye see—I was just newlins
come hame fae Barreldykes, an' there may be a sen' back for me
ony minute—there's nae kennin' fat may happen—I'll awa'
owre the road again.'

She evidently did not want to do this too hastily, nor had
Johnnie much disposition to let her, until intercommunings had
taken place. So he interjected diplomatically—'He's just on's feet
gaen awa' 'oman—come awa' ben.'

'Aweel, gin ye *wull* insist on a body; but I'm sure it's nae gweed menners to come in an' fowk i' the hoose.'

'Come yer wa's ben to the bow cheer here, till I convoy him to the closshead.'

'Wow na, John, for ye maun be sair deen oot aifter sic a day's wark—Gweed nicht wi' ye.'

'Weel, I *am* geylies forfochten. Gweed nicht, an' haste ye back.'

Wedded life seems to be a sort of forbidden ground with the story-teller, in so far, at least, as the principal characters in his story are concerned. And we readily give our adherence to the prevailing principle, which, no doubt, has its foundation in the general 'fitness of things'. For if they who enter into that sacred relationship have not first acquired a tolerably distinct conception alike of what they themselves *are* in this mundane scene, in relation to other human beings with whom they are nearly associated; and of what they must be prepared to curb and forego of selfishnesses, major and minor (and oftenest the latter, let us hope, but these often in any case) in consideration of the assured sympathy and deep unbroken confidence which the human heart, in all ordinary cases, will one time or other crave—unless it be so, the revelation of those petty disappointments, collisions of temper, and general friction of the conjugal yoke, which sometimes happen, would prove a rather humiliating and not edifying contrast to the ecstatic condition that went before, and which in such instances must seem now to be but too like 'the baseless fabric of a vision'. Happily it usually turns out to be not quite so bad as that—there is a considerably substantial 'rack' left behind. It is not quite seemly, perhaps, and it would distress the good natured story-teller immensely, to reveal to us the bride, scarce over the honeymoon, pouting, or in tears at the brutal conduct of her newly wedded husband, and he hectoring away under a fancied notion of the necessity of keeping rule as the 'head of the house'—which notion will be corrected in due time —until it ends in young madam threatening to return to her Mamma with the burden of her griefs—perhaps actually carrying out her threat, and leaving the 'head of the house' in a decidedly foolish position, till maternal wisdom and experience interpose and set matters straight again. Positively it would be cruel to call for a narration of all this; the more particularly as it will all by and by settle down into that decent, prudent, humdrum style of existence, which the persons most directly interested are content to accept in lieu of the vaguely defined Elysium into which they had seemed to themselves to be entering, but which they now believe to be a complete illusion. And in thus believing, they are just as far astray in the one direction as they previously were in the other.

It is quite possible to contract marriage on the sublimest sentiment theoretically—and land in the Divorce Court with wonderful celerity. So if we have not some decent acquaintance with what is in ourselves, and strive without fail to contribute the best we have day by day to the mutual compact we are likely to find the general result, but a sorry affair. On the contrary, where the essential qualities indicated exist, high-flown sentiment may to a considerable extent very safely give place to common sense, and yet marriage be what it was meant to be in this imperfect state of existence. And so with the two persons whose wedding has now been recorded—It would be absurd to claim for either, qualities unusually striking either morally or intellectually. But both had known somewhat of that real life experience which comes when you can no longer lean upon another, but must think and act for yourself in what is to decide your own course, and where the question must also be considered in the light of its bearing on the interests of others. And on neither had such experience, and its attendant reflections and difficulties, been thrown away.

We shall only add that Agnes has not, so far as we know, seen cause to repent her course—albeit, as regards world's 'gear', her husband, in sober truth, has never reached one whit further than Solomon's golden mean, of being neither rich nor poor. As the active, useful, and intelligent wife of a respectable and unpretending trafficker in the burgh of Strathaven, she is apparently contented, cheerful, and happy, in the performance of the quiet round of those common-place duties which lie near to us all, if we would but see it; and the right performance of which tends so greatly to the welfare of all about us, and the right ongoing of society. She has fulfilled a mother's part well to the child of her deceased friend and companion, Elsie Graham, and to Robert Morris has proved, what every true wife should be, a doubling of thought in conception, and of power in execution, for all that is good and useful in a not unworthy, nor ill-spent life.

And what of Thomas Crabbice, does any one ask? Well, that gentleman got married to a pious young lady, of an evangelical family, and qualified for the J.P. Bench in due season; and the nation has had the benefit of his enlightened judgment on all such matters as come before that judicatory—the cattle plague included —for he is assiduous in discharge of public duty; and has at various times figured as 'ruling elder' for the burgh in the great ecclesiastical Assembly—In short, he is a highly exemplary citizen; and in so far as he is known to the public, seems to bid very fair for heaven—which he intends to reach—ultimately. What his antecedents may do for him, and the prayers of the human hearts that yet cry for vengeance for wrong done, unatoned, and unrepented of—and how far he is building what will stand the inevitable test, in his vulgar, ruthless use of the power which the mere possession of money gives him in his business transactions, to over-reach and oppress the poor and less fortunate for his own aggrandisement—all such problems, if they have ever perplexed us, we must leave to an after solution.

GLOSSARY

a' all
abeen above
adee to do
afore before
agley squint, at odds
ain own
ain a-dees problems
aise ash
an' and
ance erran' on set purpose
ane one
aneuch enough
auld old
aw I
aye always
ayont beyond

baikie stake
bailie burgh magistrate
bairns children
baith both
beadle church officer
behadden beholden
birsle toast
blastin' a stroke
bleed blood
bletherin' garrulous
bode offer
body bulk in their entirety
boord board
bow cheer armchair
bowden't swollen
brae hill
braid broad

branks shackles, or bridle
bread' breadth
breeder brother
breeks trousers
breet brute
brocht brought
bun' bound

ca' push or sell
cadger hawker, carter
cam came
canna can't
carl man
caul cold
caulker a bumper
cawpable capable
choppie shop
claes clothes
claik gossip
claith cloth
clamjamfrae group
claivers, claverin' idle talk, gossiping
closs close
clown cloven
clyps gossip
compleen complain
conter against
coorse course
couper dealer
cour get the better of
craig neck, throat
cud could
cuist cast

daachter daughter
dae as we dow do what we can
dale deal
daumer't dazed
daursay daresay
debush't debauched
deein' dying
deil devil
deed indeed
deemie woman
deen done
dinna do not
doddit hornless
dogs levers
doitet silly
donallies tumblers
doon-sit establishment
doot doubt
dother daughter
drouth thirst
drow fainting fit

ee eye
eely oil
eese use
eleyvn eleven

fader father
fan when
fat what
far ben favoured
farrer further
feint devil a
fesh bring
fit foot
fleep flatterer
fley't flinched
foonry foundry
forbye besides
forehammer sledge hammer
foreneen forenoon
forfochen weary
foryet forget
fraucht supply
freens friends, relations
fu how
fuish fetched

fusky whisky
fyles whiles
fyou few

gae go
gang go
gate direction, manner, way
gaun going
gawpus fool
gedder gather
geet child
gin if
gleyed squint
gowd gold
gow't owre persuaded
grat wept
'greein' agreeing
groat coin of small denomination
grun ground
gryte great
gweed God, good

hae have
haein' having
hail whole
hain save
haiver speak nonsense
halloch thoughtless
hame home
hame drauchtit self seeking
han' hand
harns brains
haud hold
hearse hoarse
hebbit habit
heely wait
heich high
heicher higher
herrial robbery, extortion
het hot
hirstling fidgeting
hoo how
howdie midwife
howff meeting place
howffin young idiot
howp hope
howsomever however

i' the furth outside
ilka every
ill badly
ill-faur't ill-favoured
ill-guidet thoughtless
ill-wile't ill-matched
'imleen alone
immedantly immediately
Ingies the Indies
ironeery goor rusty scum
ither other
itherweese otherwise

jeel jelly
jiner joiner
jist just
jockteleg knife
joodges judges

keep's an exclamation
ken know
kin' kind
knackin' snapping
kwintra country
kye cattle

lamiter cripple
lang long
lat let
lave remainder
laverocks larks
lear knowledge, learning
leeberal liberal
lift sky
linkit joined
lip-girn snaffle
loons boys
lug ear
luik look

maingie crowd
mair more
maister master
manna must not
meeserable miserable
micht might
mink noose
min's reminds

mislippen mistrust
mither mother
mithna might not
mony many
muckle much, big
mutchkin measure of spirits
my certy an exclamation

na'ar nearly
nae no
naething nothing
naig horse
nain own
nane none
nearhaun nearly
nedder neither
neist next
neive fist
newlins newly
no not
noo now

o' of
obleeged obliged
'oman woman
on-freely bulky
oonexpeckit unexpected
oorsell ourself
oot out
owre over, too

pairis parish
pairt part
peer poor
pint point
plenishing household gear
poinding seizing a debtor's assets
potestatur prime
powney pony

quaet quiet
queetikins gaiters

raiks matters
raith a term
redd clean out
reef roof
richt very, proper

riggit striped
rizzon reason
roun'/roon round

sair serve, painful, painfully
sanna shall not
sax six
scaup bare open ground
scoondrel scoundrel
seer sure
seerly surely
settin comely
shalt pony
shealin sids grain husks
sheen shoes
shirra sherriff
sic such
siller money
sin son
sittivation job
skaim scheme
skweel school
sloom rumour
slype low fellow
sma' small
smore smother
snod neat
sonsy buxom
sorra sorrow
splore trick, prank
spreein' debauchery
squar-wrichtin joiner work
stank ditch
stap step
starshie turmoil, commotion
steed stood
steekit clenched
stock man
store the kin survive
streen, the streen yesterday evening
stoupie small container
sud should
suddenty suddenness
syne then

ta'en through han' handled
tane one
tauld told
tee too
thigged cadged
thocht thought
thole endure, suffer
thooms thumbs
thrawart perverse
tocher dowry
toitlin toddling
toon town
traivel travel
tribblet troubled
twa two
tyce entice
tyeuch tough

ugsome repulsive
umquhile former
up-by-cairts prosperous

verra very
vizzy view

wake weak
walthy wealthy
ware spend
wark work
warl/warld world
warst worst
waur worse
wechty moggin heavy purse
weel well
weel-a-wat an exclamation
whan when
whase whose
wheesht be silent
wi' with
wile vile
wudna would not

yammer repeat noisily
ye you